Life,
Hope, and
Forgiveness

Life, Hope, and Forgiveness

A Journey of Self Discovery

D.G. CRABBE

Printed in the United States of America

First Printing, 2020

ISBN: 978-1-64746-376-2 (Paperback)
ISBN: 978-1-64746-377-9 (Hardback)
ISBN: 978-1-64746-378-6 (eBook)

Front cover image by
Book design by

Library of Congress Control Number (LCCN): 2020123456

www.whateveryoururlis.com

To my beloved JC, the rock I still lean on...

Contents

Disclaimer

I have tried to recreate events, locales, and conversations from my memories of them. In order to maintain their anonymity, in some instances, I have changed the names of individuals and places; I may have changed some identifying characteristics and details such as physical properties, occupations, and places of residence.

Preface

Are you willing to change? Are you ready to transform your life? If you have this book in hand, there must be a reason. Your life isn't complete, and you are looking for something to push you in the right direction. Or you bought it simply because you liked the cover. Or the name of the book appealed to you.

I'm not a guru, scientist, psychiatrist, or saviour; I'm just one person with her life, ideas, mistakes, characteristics, behaviours, and values. I have done what I thought was best for myself, and I have made lots of mistakes. A human mind specialist would say I have been impacted by what I saw in my family and in my childhood.

Being a woman doesn't help much. Women are sensitive and understanding; we have a side that allows us to easily see the pain and suffering in others. We are emphatic about other people's problems, and we help when we can. But we are blind towards our own troubles; we have no sympathy for ourselves. How many times have you helped a stranger—male or female? How many times have you listened to a friend's difficulties and put all your heart into helping this friend? And then, when you're having trouble with something, how often do you keep it to yourself? Self-denial is a natural form of self-protection. It is easier for you to accept your own pain, whatever form this pain has—trouble with family, love, friends, job, or money.

My book is called <u>Life, Hope, and Forgiveness</u> for a reason. I have lived my *life* for 44 years, my own way. I had good and bad moments. I struggled. I was happy, or I lied to myself that I was. I helped others, but I didn't know I needed help too. I loved, mostly, wrong men. I hated, and I didn't want to hear about *forgiveness*. I didn't love myself, or I didn't know how to. And I was sure I didn't deserve better things in my *life*. I lied to make things look better for me. I have done right and wrong things, but I *hoped* that one day I'd be able to see the light; that something good would happen to me. And I don't mean good in terms of finances, I mean good in terms of consciousness.

Do you see yourself in some of my words?

I have always measured the depth of my love by the degree of the pain a relationship had. I followed the same pattern I saw at home as a child, with my mother giving so much love to a man who loved her, but, at the same time, gave her so much pain, especially when he was drinking. I was sure love meant torment and difficulties. I tried the best I could to fix everything that went wrong, and I became a caregiver to needy, emotionally unavailable men. If a relationship failed, I took all the blame. I was not good enough; I was not sufficient. I didn't consider if the man was reliable and right for me. I was more in touch with the dream of the situation than with reality, and I lost the one essential, most important thing: **me**.

Our world is filled with torment and pain. We continuously struggle for something, and fear of the future appears as a standard part of our lives. We continue to do a job we don't like out of fear we won't be able to pay bills. Or we fear someone else will take the job. So we work long hours at home, just to appear a saint in the boss' eyes. We give in and please our partners out of fear we will lose them.

We think of others, of how to please the world, and we let ourselves down. I have done it. Our lives are different, but we all have similar problems, and we don't love ourselves enough. We want love, money, a specific social position, a grand house, a beautiful body, health, or happiness, but we forget the soul. We are consumed by our thoughts, using them to punish ourselves for our own negative actions in the past. We self-broadcast bad movies about an anxious future or compare ourselves to others who have achieved more with or in their lives.

We seem so keen on focussing on small fragments of our lives and not on the whole picture. The stress eats at us, we are unhappy when things don't work how we want, we feel like victims, and we blame life. We think life is always cruel to us. We spend too much time victimising ourselves, with all negative thinking that we nourish our minds with.

It can be a challenge to try something radically different. When I thought I had enough of my life the way it was, the hardest thing, for me, was to recognise I had a problem. But once I did this, nothing could stop. I surrendered. I, mentally, rooted out my hurts, realising what kept my mind in the dark. You need to name your issues if you want freedom from them.

I realised I had a choice—to accept my life the way it was until now or to let go of the past and learn to heal my soul. I learned to love myself and worked through the sadness, pain, and resentment of my past. To embrace a healthy and enjoyable experience, learning to forgive—myself first, then after, others. I still hold some grudges, but I had enough strength to forgive.

Now I understand the importance of mindfulness and forgiveness to heal myself.

In this book, I will give you a glimpse into my life; maybe some of you will recognise yourself in various lines of my story. This is my way of overcoming hate and hurt: let go of old baggage and move on from the past. This became my approach to growing as a healthy and happy person.

This is a self-help book and includes my personal three steps to recovering. I don't demand you do the same. It is just a mere suggestion. And I hope someone will take advantage of my path: forgiving without forgetting, genuinely living without resentment, and liberating yourself.

My healing process includes tools everyone can use to break free from the heavy chain of the past.

Move forward, read on, and I hope you find something inside my story that inspires you.

> "For in every adult there dwells the child that was, and in every child there lies the adult that will be."
> John Connolly, *The Book of Lost Things*

CHAPTER 1

God and Devil

Will he survive this terrible illness? Will he be smiling tomorrow? Life and death are the only concerns my mind has right now.

I'll be 49 years old in two weeks, but my date of birth is not relevant during this time of pain. I am near his bed—for the last two months, this bed has been only his bed—and I am holding his skinny hand, trying to give him some positive energy. During these last two months, he has started to refuse food, and last week was even worse. I am happy only because he drinks Lucozade (an energy drink) or San Pellegrino water. I can see him fading day by day, and I feel a knot in my stomach that has found its home there.

My heart is in pieces, and I wonder what would have happened to me without:

- Meditation—working in mindfulness,

- YouTube audio files and books about spiritual enlightenment—to keep my mind occupied,

- The colleagues from my online business platform,

- The right friends—Johanna, who appeared at my door, every time I was at a breaking point, crying and feeling lost,

- My willingness to change and improve the way I see life— JC showed me I am strong, willing to change, and ready to see life from a new perspective.

My wonderful husband, JC, is lying in bed, and every time I enter the room, I feel all my heart filling with love. Five years ago, I met him, and there was not a single moment when I could not perceive this warmth. He radiates joy, happiness, love, and intelligence. He is my rock! Because of him, I am a new, positive person. He's an excellent teacher, yes, but I was like clay awaiting the magic of the potter's hands.

Every hour, I tempt him with the food he used to love. Sometimes, he refuses to eat, but he remembers to take my hand and hold it warmly. It is his way of apologizing for refusing to eat. I know he loves me. Even while ill, he is trying not to hurt my feelings. I ask him if he's in pain, and he answers, "I have to keep you happy, not upset you."

I know the tears are coming, and I use needing to visit the toilet as an excuse to leave the room. Near the bed, I wonder what will happen to me if JC gets worse. I am trying to be realistic with myself. I am loved, and I love, we have respect for each other, we are laughing a lot, and playing like children.

These years have been some of the best times of my life! There was a time confusion was my home, and I was never happy for very long. It was a mix of sweet and horrendous days, months, and years where I was sure I did not deserve, perhaps, something better in my life.

I was born in a small village in Transylvania, land of mystery and beauty, where people used to meet on cold winter nights near a fire, telling scary stories. These meetings happened frequently, when the Communist regime shut down the power for hours, usually between 6 pm and 10 pm.

They wanted to teach us to preserve everything, from food to electricity; by taking it away. But they could never take hope from the souls of people.

I lived with my parents, Lucy and George, and my uncle, Trajan, in my granny's old house. There was no living room or common area, only a long corridor with doorways to various rooms.

My granny's name was Mica. Her chamber was the place to conduct the daily chores. I noticed two other doors, but they were locked. I was always inquisitive. The adults didn't let me enter either of the two rooms. For my own safety, of course. Regardless, I found the keys, and I explored everything. I almost broke a leg in the first room, which was full of furniture. The second room was a kind of fridge for ham and sausages. Knowing how much I liked meat, the adults supposed I would go there with a knife in hand and hurt myself.

The first memory I have is the moment I made my first steps; my mother said I was nine months old. My mother and I were in the long corridor in opposite corners, and I was crawling around a small table. Something interesting was on top, and I wanted to grab it. My mother changed her pouting face into a smiling one, watching me try to walk.

"Come to me!" My mom tried to persuade me to walk to her.

I almost ran towards her; she was waiting with open arms for my arrival. My father appeared from another room. He spoke to someone inside the room, telling them to come to see his daughter walking. He took me in his arms. He cuddled me and made me laugh.

We were now eye-to-eye, and I felt so much love. His eyes were dark, almond-shaped, with long black lashes, on a starkly white face with red lips. I put my hand in his curly, brown hair, and I was astonished by the beauty I saw. This feeling was fleeting. I then noticed something I did not like. His breath was strange, his voice too loud, his beautiful eyes had a malicious glimmer in them. I felt uncomfortable. In my little mind, I linked my mother's pouting face with my father's actions. Though my father was still cuddling me, he knew I was not happy with something.

"Why is she watching me like this? Did you teach her that too? It was enough with one; now, I have to stand two ugly faces!" My father snarled.

Mom took me into her arms; we went outside the house. My father returned to his friends, I supposed, telling them some funny story. For the rest of my life, when he drank, he refused to look into my eyes. He said my look was hurting his soul. He was hurting mine too.

I grew, and I remember my mother working. When she wasn't cleaning the house—Trajan Jr. helped when he could—she was knitting or doing some other handcraft.

My father also loved to make beautiful things—carving and painting.

Every Sunday, my father, who enjoyed the fresh air, took us to the river to fish. The river was three kilometres from our village, and we walked to get there. During the trip to the river, he told us stories. Stories about sports or hunting—both of these pastimes my father enjoyed. I could listen for days and not be bored. He was so funny!

I was an angler; I had my little tools, and I desired to make my father proud. I wanted the fishing hooks, and I was lucky to have them. My hooks were always full of small fish. There were anglers all along the riverbank, waiting for a fish to take their bait. We were still lucky, fishing for something. My father knew what to use as bait. Boys from the village came to see him, and they wanted to learn from him. He was their idol, and they adored him.

We were living under a Communist regime, and there were lots of rules to be followed. Because of all this, people liked to eat the fish we caught in the river. People got protein from the fish, as we were not provided with enough meat, bread, sugar, or rice.

One day, a technician came to repair the TV. He said, "Is dead, never will work again." Yet he continued to try to fix it; I watched him opening the box and doing his job. I liked the TV, and I wasn't happy with this answer. I was a curious four-year-old, and I could not resist; I needed to see for myself what was inside this box.

My uncle was an electrician, too, and I had seen his tools. I took one of his screwdrivers, and I started working.

Suddenly, loud voices erupted from the TV. All the family rushed to the room, frightened by the noise, and then by me, with the screwdriver in hand, behind the box, risking electrocution. They began shouting at me. I wept all night.

They were happy about the TV working again but worried about what could have happened to me. They talked for months about this, until something else happened.

My granny noticed that 90% of the time, when I turned on the lights, the bulbs exploded. The weird thing was, it only happened to me; no one in the family could explain why. I remember I used to turn the lights off and on repeatedly when I was in a bad mood because my family refused me something. My father used to joke I had a strange power, but I used it to do damage instead of helping. They did not like to beat me, but I was often punished—put in a corner, facing the wall—for long periods of time.

My father was a veterinarian (vet), and people from the village and beyond, even from 30-40 km away, came for help. They loved him and trusted him. I understood later what kind of relief they wanted.

Our president, at the time, after an encounter with another dictator, decided Romanians were too fat, and they needed a strict diet. He put a law in place, so everyone had rationed food: x grams of meat, salami, bread, rice, sugar, etc. per month.

The government sent brigades to every village to count the number of animals (for meat) in each household; these brigades kept a close eye on pregnant animals.

My father, being the vet, assisted with births, especially for cows. Peasants tried declaring newborn cows dead. To do this, my father needed to sign a death certificate; thus, his signature was very precious to people.

Lots of people did not have enough money and needed to eat. By declaring these newborns dead, these households could eat the meat and the government would not notice.

Risking his job, and his life, my father gave a hand to each poor family asking for this help. He was their only hope to feed their family.

He did the same for us, his own family.

I always asked for meat; I did not like vegetables. Meat, fish, milk, cream, and cakes were my favourites. Somehow, my father provided what we liked. He provided us with money and food.

My mother took care of the house and raised the animals. She was a great worker but still sensitive, and with an artistic bone.

I had, again, done something to upset my mother, who was now pregnant with my sister.

There was a strange man, from another village, helping in the garden. He was small, with a woman's shape. His hips were wide, and he wore a suit that looked too big for him.

I was only a child, but I could see something wasn't right with him. He was mentally disabled. But he was a very hard worker. 'George, the Mad' was what the villagers called him.

He was digging in the garden when my mother called out to him, "George, would you please bring me a bucket of water from the well? I am pregnant, and I don't feel very well."

"No, it isn't my fault you're pregnant. It wasn't me who made you pregnant. Ask your husband," answered the mad man.

My mom was red in the face—angry.

At that moment, I was playing on the terrace, and I broke the vase my mother had cleaned for fresh flowers. It was only a vase, but it was an heirloom. She received it from her mother, and it held precious memories.

All day long, I seemed to have done only stupid things, one after another.

Mom appeared at the door holding a handbag with some of my clothes inside and two apples. "I am sending you to the world. I want you to leave the house. You are a bad girl, and I don't want you anymore," she stated.

I took the handbag and started to leave. I walked until the trees were covering the view of the house, then I began to cry. I did not like the world. I was a little girl, and I didn't want to be alone.

"She doesn't love me! What am I to do now?" I asked myself.

The backyard was, for me, a big, scary world where the 'black man,' 'the ugly witch,' or even a wolf could eat me.

Suddenly, my father appeared, took my hand, cuddled me, and began to guide me towards the car.

"No one can send my baby girl away. Dad loves you; he won't let you down; he will take care of you forever," he told me as he hugged me and placed me in his car.

He went to the house to make sure my mother was fine. He then politely asked George to help my mom with anything she needed. Dad gave George some money. Now George went promptly to the well, ready to get Mom her water.

My father took me with him to the next village where he had to do a job. I think he wanted to let mom relax. I was so happy. He was my hero!

With my mother pregnant, I often went out with my father. Sometimes he took me on his black motorbike—I loved the speed and the wind hitting my face.

My father told me one day that we would have a house near granny soon. To do this, we needed to go buy bricks from the gypsies working near the cemetery.

I was thrilled by their lifestyle. The kids walked around the camp, barefoot. They were dirty, and no one was arguing with them. I didn't see any tables or plates around, yet food was cooking on top of the fire—which was in a big pit in the ground. I ate with them; the food tasted wonderful. They had puppies with them. I wanted to sleep there. Instead, Dad promised me he would buy me a dog. Then we went home.

I did not understand why, for three days after, my mother checked my long hair for hours at a time. She wanted to make sure I hadn't caught anything from the gypsy camp.

Two days after that, my father brought home a dog. It was not a puppy, but I was in love! I forgot my cat, who had been like a sister to me. Instead, I knew I would love dogs forever. The dog, Blitz, was a dark-coloured German Shepherd and was trained by the police. He had an accident, and the police surrendered him to my father—to keep or put down.

Blitz stayed near me every moment. If I tried to leave the yard and closed the gate, Blitz would climb over the gate and push me back in the yard. "*Oh, God, I have another boss!*" I thought. I went to school every morning. At noon, when the church bells sounded, Blitz was on the front step, waiting for me. He took my little bag in his mouth and would push me near the fence. He was protecting me from the cars. I was so proud. Now I had a dog who would be like a brother.

I was a bit worried because Mom was becoming very fat. She told me soon I would have a sister, but I didn't understand why her belly was so big.

The day she went to the hospital, Dad was placing me in my bed as he explained, "Mom went to buy you a sister. She will need time to find you a good sister, but don't worry; she will be home soon. Be kind and listen to Mica."

"I want milk!" I cried, somewhat oblivious to the situation at hand.

Dad was in a hurry and poured milk in a small glass—one of the ones he used for alcohol. I took it in my hands, but I didn't want to drink from it. Dad became a monster after he drank from these small glasses. My granny, Mica, took the full glass from my hands after a while.

"I don't like monsters." I thought to myself, *"but I am thirsty."* So, I drank the milk in the end.

My mother was still 'shopping' for my sister three days later. I could feel the tension in the air at the house. I didn't want a sister anymore; I only wanted my beautiful, sweet Mom back.

Dad took me to the hospital, eventually, where I could see my little sister. I saw a kind of aquarium with two holes where you fit your hands inside fitted gloves. You were only allowed to touch the baby with them on. They were all watching the baby, but I could not see her at first. My father took me in his arms and lifted me up. Surprise! Inside that box of glass, there was a small, dark creature with long, straight, black hair.

"That thing is a hedgehog, not a sister!" I thought.

Unable to smile, I realized I didn't want this ugly, dark creature to be my sister. Everybody else was amazed by the little creature.

I felt lost. I was losing my position of 'only child' in the family.

After some months, 'the hedgehog' came home (she was born prematurely, at seven months) and she was slowly transforming in a beautiful little sister. I wondered how the ugly hedgehog could be so pretty now. She had black eyes and hair, and I wanted to kiss her every minute. I knew now there was space for both of us in our family. She cried a lot. Blitz was there for me; he kept me company. We were busy all day long.

I liked to be the princess of the house, and my uncle, Trajan Jr. (the electrician), did anything and everything to make me happy. He was dating, and often met ladies on Sunday at a lovely restaurant in the middle of a beautiful forest. The women often bought me juices and sweets, and I felt happy there. The best part was the trip on my uncle's bicycle; I would hang on the bicycle handlebars, with my arms around his neck. He was such a wonderful uncle; I loved him.

At home, he had another surprise for me. He poured hot water—boiled on the top of my granny's stove—in a wooden tub, and for two hours, no one could take me out of this heavenly tub. He never said he was too tired to do this for me. For years, he set up this improvised bathtub, only to make me happy.

One day he had another surprise for me. He knew I loved eating ham. He opened one of the two closed doors that I wasn't allowed into—Mica's room. Smoked sausages and bacon hung from the ceiling; I was in heaven.

I observed where the key was kept, and I started going there lots of times on my own, with a chair and a knife in hand. The chair was for climbing to reach the ham. Of course, I was caught and got in trouble because of the blade in my hand.

My curiosity had gotten the better of me—as my granny and parents had expected.

The family was getting ready to baptize my sister, the little princess, who was now one. There was to be a party afterwards. At the party, there was lots of socializing—greetings, laughing, and talking.

I was playing outside with a friend. She was curious about something happening in the house.

My father was in the hall, drunk, trying to hit someone. My mother tried to talk to him, but he was pushing her away, calling her names. My friend approached the door to hear better. Her big, wide eyes took in the movie my father was offering for free.

He saw her watching, so he came out and kicked her bottom with his sharp shoes. She could not stand the pain and ran home in tears.

I froze; I felt I would die from the shame.

I hate Dad. *She was only a child; why was he so mean?* I felt ashamed of him. This moment still haunts me.

Our new house was ready for us, but there was no furniture inside. My granny gave us a table and chairs as well as some other furniture. Day by day, new pieces of furniture appeared. Soon we had two rooms and the kitchen ready. The rooms had big windows and were spacious. We were happy in this place.

My parents worked hard. Soon we had the house and yard decorated. The garden showcased plenty of colourful life, with various flowers, fruit, trees, and vegetables. The neighbours were amazed by my mother's exquisite taste. In a few years, we had the most beautiful house in the village. My mom was taking care of the home and animals. We had a lot of animals. These animals were sold, and more money came into the household.

While Mom was busy with the household, my father was doing his job as a vet. In the evenings, the yard and house were full of people looking for my father. Some wanted help for themselves. Some were boys who wanted to see him/spend time with him or to give a hand with chores around the house. Dad was drawing, painting, and carving; every day, he created fantastic things. He and the boys were laughing and having fun. The boys adored him. I was very proud of him but jealous at the same time. I thought maybe he would have liked to have a boy.

I noticed, when going with Dad to his job, people wanted to give him something in return for his help. They would often have a regional, sweet or salty pie or homemade alcohol on the table. They may not have had a lot of food, but every backyard was full of fruit trees, and people made all kinds of alcoholic drinks from the fruit. When you entered a house, you needed to taste the pie and drink the entire beverage. It was customary. If you didn't, it was believed you left nasty luck in their home.

Dad was always in a hurry, wanting to help as many people as possible. He had not time to eat, but he could drink quickly and then move on. He started to drink almost every day, and it was hell at home.

Within his goodness and willingness to help others, his destruction took hold.

When drunk, he would shout at my mother. He refused food, and I saw dishes, full of food, flying around the living room.

My mother was suffering and became very lonely. She hid in the house, working, avoiding her girlfriends. I supposed the people around had heard and seen my father when he was drunk. They knew what he was doing and how violent he could be, but no one ever said anything when I was a child.

I learned to hide my father's alcoholic side from other new friends and acquaintances because I knew he was unpleasant when he drank. I felt immense love for him, but I wanted him to change. I tried to treat my mother better—helping her more, making her smile, and doing everything I could to help.

But I was a child, I wanted to play, to go to the river for a swim, and to do all the things other children were doing. The teenagers from the neighbourhood called on Mom often, to learn her new models of knitting or some unique skill in needlework. She smiled and seemed happy when she was with them. She felt appreciated.

✒

My father was now a hunter and carried a gun for hunting. He had lots of friends in his new group. Every Sunday, they met and traversed outside the village to hunt. He came home with pheasants, rabbits, or wild ducks. I was delighted because I loved meat. The hunter's group stopped by our house, and I knew I would like to be part of their group. Sometimes they asked Mom to cook a rabbit in red wine—that was like a party for me. The smell in the house was so inviting I felt I would die if the food was not ready quickly enough.

When there was too much food, Mom gave the surplus to my granny, neighbours, or friends.

Once my father came home from fishing with a huge fish—12 kg. He invited all the kids around the neighbourhood to eat. He put a long table outside, and there were about 15 boys and girls who enjoyed a tasty meal.

✒

Blitz died when I was five years old, and I wept every day and night because I lost my best friend.

Mica told me, "Blitz went to be with God. He will be happy in heaven."

"God? Why did Blitz prefer God to me? And who is this God that wants my friend?" I asked my granny.

"God is the creator of everything you see and touch, and you need to pray to him every night before you go to sleep to help you to grow healthy. Didn't your mother teach you this?" Mica asked me with a frown on her face.

"I don't understand God, and I don't want to pray. Mom said I don't need to see God; I only need to believe in Him because He created all of us. She said, 'He is good and kind, and He will protect us.' But I don't like this God!" I blurted out confrontationally.

"Goodness gracious me! What are you talking about?" Mica asked.

"If God is who you say, an all-powerful being, he would not let Dad keep drinking!" I stated angrily.

I could see she was upset by my words, and we had a long chat about this topic. She told me there was a Devil too, and we must behave because if we didn't, the Devil would take us instead, and we would burn in a big fire, in immense pain.

I was flummoxed. If God was the powerful one, why did He let the Devil do whatever the Devil liked? Why didn't God stop the Devil? Why didn't God help Dad stop drinking? People seemed to think God was powerful, but it appeared to me that God couldn't stop Devil!

Then I grasped why Dad drank—he liked the Devil. That's what I thought anyway.

All this thinking had given me a headache. I still did not understand why God would take Blitz from me. I reckoned, *"This God isn't my friend!"*

At six years old, I started school in the village. I learned everything quickly. As soon as I knew the alphabet, I tried to read books. I clutched them in my hand, as one would a precious gem. In fact, I often forgot to eat or play with friends.

Mom was happy with my interest in books. I was keeping busy. But she did not want the books on the table when we ate. So, I learned to eat in a hurry.

The first book I found in my mother's library was *Legends of the Olympus*. I loved all the stories, but I did not like Zeus very much. He was too elusive and manipulative for my taste. I was passionate about books. I read *Pride and Prejudice*, *Jane Eyre*, *The Galsworthy Family*, *Great Expectations*, *Anna Karenina*, *Crime and Punishment*, *Gone with the Wind*, *Rebecca*, *Les Misérables*, *Wuthering Heights*, and lots more. I adored books.

My mother was a bit worried about all this reading. I read all the time when I was not at school.

"One day, I will have a book with my name on it!" I told her one day.

"Okay. The first to read it will be me." She smiled, and we talked for hours about the book I was reading at the time.

I wanted her to be proud of me. I loved her so much.

When my sister was two years old, she was a little dolly. She liked gorgeous dresses, and she would not put on something she didn't like.

She was always trying to get me into trouble; I did not like this very much. If I was talking with my girlfriends, she reported everything at home. It was annoying! I just wanted my freedom.

One time, I was going to swim in the river with friends, but they thought it was too risky to go with me because of my sister's tattling. My parents had forbidden the trip to the river without one of them because every year someone died swimming there. I went anyway; I was naughty.

We were sharing a room, toys, food, a bed—everything. I wanted time for myself, but my sister would cry when I hid from her.

I was not pleasant to her all the time, but I would never let anyone harm her. I loved her despite all the trouble she got me into.

My father helped me with my homework, especially math. He explained the problem logically and let me do the work. When he did not like my writing or answers or something else, he ripped the page out. Page after page flew from my notebook, and got torn up. I made lots of mistakes at first. For a month, I had to use a new notebook every day.

"You aren't good enough! You need to concentrate more on what you are doing," he told me, repeatedly.

I knew he was right, but I wanted to do what I liked, and I liked to read, not do math. But Dad continued to push me along in the right direction.

I worked hard and excelled at school.

One day, my colleagues' parents came to the class, sat for two hours, and watched us. I was somewhat jealous, as I did not understand why my parents were not there.

The teacher did her job as usual, and I forgot the audience because I was really involved. I loved literature and reading. During reading class, I knew all the answers, so I interacted a lot. Then we had math, and the teacher gave us five or six problems to solve. I was ready 15 minutes before anyone else. Thanks to my dad's instruction, I was better than any of my colleagues.

Once at home, I heard my parents talking. Apparently, other parents had accused the teacher that she preferred me to other scholars. So, this teacher wanted to show them all what happened in the class in real-time.

After that day in class, I noticed the people in the village treated me differently; this was not a good feeling. I was not a prodigy child; I studied. A lot. I enjoyed aspects of school. Dad spent a lot of his free time helping me with my homework, and this is contributed to my success.

At home, things were flowing smoothly for weeks or even months. My father did not touch alcohol, and life was just what should be—a fantastic journey, coloured with love and happiness.

Dad gave me all the support I needed. He started spending more time with the family—teaching me how to draw and taking us fishing. He even taught me to swim. Soon, I began helping him when he operated on animals—as his assistant. I planted my first tree with him, and I learned to grow tomatoes, peppers, cucumbers, aubergines, and other vegetables.

All the family was happy.

I received my first bicycle, and he was there, helping me every moment.

When he came home from work, he would have some pleasant surprise—like a nice crusty loaf, still hot from the oven; some freshly made sausages; a piece of ham; or chocolate. Even when he was drunk, he came home with goodies.

In a world of poverty, we never were hungry. Meat was supplied from hunting. Friends provided us with other items. One day, a friend of my dad's gave us four big containers full of different types of honey. This was a treat because, in the Communist shops, sugar could not be found. Then, for days, he was drinking again. The plates with food were back to flying across the living room; my mother was terrified and tired. She took to hiding in the garden. I noticed bruises on her face and body. Ones she could not hide.

My sister and I were still playing— trying to avoid these moments in the best way we could. We did not talk about Dad's behaviour. It was like it never happened. I kept this pain in my heart. I was cautious not to answer my neighbours' questions. This shame was to stay in the house.

I still loved my father immensely, but some days, I wanted him to disappear. Words were not enough to describe pain in my heart. I lived in constant fear. When he did not drink, I never wanted the day to end. Those days were beautiful and quiet, and we were happy. But then, the next day, he could come home drunk.

Even now, the thought of this is making me sick. I jump when I hear men speaking loudly. I cannot control my reaction. Sometimes I become breathless, and my heart pounds crazily.

From the time I was six until I turned 10, I had the same four dreams.

In the first, I was climbing a long ladder. It felt like I was doing this all night long. When I got to the top, someone pushed the ladder from the wall. At that instant, I thought I was going to die, but I woke up at the last moment, sweating and shivering.

In the second, I was on a plane with rows six chairs wide. I felt the speed of the plane change quickly. The aeroplane would disintegrate, and I would freefall in the air, chained to a chair, speeding up as I fell further. I would awake before my body impacted the ground.

The third was very crazy. All night I would be jumping like Tarzan from one rope to another. But instead of swinging tree to tree, I was on top of the clouds. The trick was to arrive in time to catch the next rope if I did not want to fall.

In the fourth, I was in a very tall building, climbing stairs. Suddenly, the protective grid disappeared, and I could not breathe, scared I would fall.

These nights were horrendous because the dreams seemed very real for me. I would wake up tired and frightened. Yet, I kept them to myself.

I didn't know, at the time, that falling in a dream represents succumbing to your insecurities and anxieties. Often, the dreamer doesn't feel they have full control of their life. And I didn't during that time of my life.

Fate was to prove yet another example of this lack of control I had in my life when Mom took my sister and me to the hospital for her check-up.

"I do not miss childhood, but I miss the way I took pleasure in small things, even as greater things crumbled. I could not control the world I was in, could not walk away from things or people or moments that hurt, but I took joy in the things that made me happy."
Neil Gaiman, *The Ocean at the End of the Lane*

CHAPTER 2

Questioning

We travelled to the city and went to the main hospital. My mother took us both with her; she did this regardless of where she was going. I did not understand why we were at the hospital, and I did not bother to ask. My sister and I enjoyed taking the bus to the city. Mom would sometimes treat us with a visit to the best coffee shop in town, where we could choose among very sophisticated cakes and juices.

Today, our visit to the shop, before we went to the hospital, was subdued. I could tell Mom's head was somewhere else. Her face was a bit sad, but she tried to appear happy despite a bruise on her cheek, which was covered with makeup. I knew something was not right. She was beautiful and thin—wearing a skirt suit that enhanced her figure. She was always elegant; I would see people on the street watching her with appreciation. I was very proud of her. She also had extraordinary kindness and never talked about others. She saw something good in everyone and helped as best she could when asked.

After the coffee shop, we went to choose shoes and clothes for my sister and I. We were even lucky enough to buy a new dolly. I was 10 at the time; my sister was six, but we still liked dolls.

The hospital was huge, and we were sent from one place to another, walking down long corridors, and changing floors often. Mom had lots of checks before she actually saw the doctor. While a nurse took blood samples, I asked Mom what was going on.

"Are you ill? Why are you doing all these tests?" I asked.

"I feel exhausted, I only want to sleep, and I am always thirsty. Maybe I need vitamins," Mom explained.

"Do I need to worry? I can…"

"No, darling, you do not need to worry at all. I am in the hospital, and they will tell me what to do." She hugged me, and I felt better.

After that, we went into a room with a doctor, Daniel. He was talking with Mom. He asked questions about her lifestyle—what she was eating, how she cooked the food, what was she doing for a living, etc. My sister and I were impressed by how cute and handsome the doctor was.

I heard the word diabetes. This was my mother's diagnosis. The doctor explained to her all about it, including what she needed to do. She was to take injectable insulin twice per day, which she would be provided in a small bag to take home. Mom rubbed her hands together but appeared calm, asking the doctor more about the new food requirements.

Even my sister showed signs of panic; I told her it would all be fine. She caressed her new dolly, but her beautiful face had a grimace on it. We knew, in our hearts, something terrible was starting, and we hoped our mother would get better. She liked sweet things and was an expert in making cakes. How would we stop her from eating them?

The doctor sent Mom with the nurse for a short course on insulin injections, and my sister went with them. The doctor asked me to sit in front of him and talk about my mother's new diet. All the family would need to help and embrace this lifestyle. He explained to me what was better to eat and how we could help Mom. I did not agree with everything he said because I loved sweets, but I understood "an ounce of prevention is worth a pound of cure." The more we prevented the outbreaks, the better.

He handed me a little book and started asking about school and life. "Your Mom told me you are very good at school. Would you like to be a teacher?"

"Oh, yes, I would like to be a teacher! Maybe a literature or language teacher. Next year I will go to another school, and I will learn new languages. I love French," I responded enthusiastically. I was happy he seemed interested in me.

"You are a nice girl, and you will marry a nice guy," he told me.

He was writing something as we spoke. I could not see his eyes because they were scrutinising the papers in front of him. Now I became upset. The words *marry,* and *a nice guy* boiled like oil on my face and heart. Without thinking, I exploded into a long tirade about men and married life.

"Marry? I will never marry! I will never be a slave. Nobody will tell me what to do, and nobody will decide for me. I want to be independent and do what I want! Men? Disgusting…" but I stopped because I understood what he was doing.

He was watching me with his big, grey eyes and calmly continued to challenge me, "Oh, you are so upset with men. Is it your father such a commander? Is he so bad?"

"No, he is lovely. My dad is amazing. He is intelligent, loves animals, paints and carves, and he is a storyteller. I think he is the most beloved man in the village. He helps lots of people and is always available to others." I rambled in my panic. I tried to smile my best smile. The doctor had tricked me, and my heart was running crazy in my little chest. I wanted fresh air. I wanted to run away, but, instead, I sat, composed, forcing myself to appear calm.

"Is your Mom gardening a lot?" he asked.

"Mmm, yes, she likes it."

"She needs to be careful. I noticed a bruise on her face. With diabetes, wounds can be dangerous," he said while keeping his eyes on the papers again.

"Sorry? Why are bruises dangerous?"

"Because diabetes impacts the body's ability to heal wounds quickly. This is a small wound, but she can't risk anything worse because it will further impact her health. All the family will need to take care of your mother. I will need to talk to your father too. I think he and my father work together sometimes. Doesn't he work at X place?"

"Oh, yes, maybe I know your father!"

He told me his father's name. I remembered him, but I did not understand what he wanted from me.

Mom came back and appeared more tired. The doctor wanted to talk to her alone, so I took my sister into the hallway. She told me Mom now has a little pistol for injections so they will be quick and won't hurt.

Mom finished with the doctor, and we travelled back home. She did not talk on the way home, and the feeling that something was wrong kept me unhappy. At home, she let us play because we were on summer vacation from school. Later she took me aside for a chat. I knew I was in trouble.

She asked me about my conversation with Daniel, "How could you tell him your father is bad? Does your father refuse you anything? You have love, food, clothes, toys, books, and a beautiful house! He does all he can to give his family what they need and want, and you tell a stranger that you are unhappy?" She looked sad and disappointed, and I started to cry.

"It wasn't like that; I swear!" I was so embarrassed. I did not know what to say to make her feel better and forget all this.

"Your father loves you and your sister, and he works to provide you with the best he can!"

I was ashamed and confused at the same time. Dad was doing all this for us, but seemed to not care for her, especially when he drank—he became a man who shouted and said mean words to her. *Is it possible she could not see this? Why was she protecting him so much? Is that what a wife must do? Is it right?*

My introspection finished because Dad arrived from work. He was delighted to be home. Just to show the irony in what I was thinking, he had gifts for us. He was laughing, and that made Mom smile. We had supper together, and Dad took Mom into the garden to plant some fruit trees. After an hour, they returned. Watching them together made me feel so guilty. They were kissing and playing like kids. Near the well, where there was a wooden tub, they splashed water on each other. Because of back pain, Dad could not wash his feet thoroughly, so Mom did it for him.

Jesus and Magdalena! I thought. *Mom is a real saint. She truly is, and he is the Devil in disguise. I am so bad. I talk too much, and I am ungrateful to my parents.*

The night passed. I kept thinking about how it was possible to love someone and hate them so much at the same time. The truth was, I did not hate *him*; I hated the alcohol and how it made him behave. I believed they were so happy together on that evening, and I needed to keep it this way. When everybody was sleeping, I went to the kitchen, found where my father put the bottle with brandy, drained it in the sink, and replaced it with water. I knew I would be in trouble for doing this, but I did not care.

The morning held pleasant surprises; the sky was clear, and my father was coming home for 10 minutes to drop off a puppy that he needed to train for hunting. It was female, brown, with long ears, a round mouth, and long legs. She was a German Sheppard and seemed to be a toy. Her name was Lola. My sister and I were thrilled; Mom cuddled and kissed her shiny head. We took Lola into the back garden. She was curious about the grass and flowers; she sneezed and jumped around. When we passed near the chickens, she entered a kind of trance. She put her tail high, held still, and lifted her right leg into the air. We were laughing, and little Lola jumped to us, licking our hands and faces. I remembered Blitz at that moment and let out a big sigh. I knew Lola would be a joy for our family, and I was happy that Dad loved dogs.

In the evening, Dad came home with lots of goodies for us, and I was happy to see ham and a fresh, hot loaf. We could not find butter in the shops, but Mom made it at home from cow's milk. She put a big jar filled with milk in the fridge—for three days—to rest. Then she would remove the cream from the top of the pot, to make butter. It was a long process because you needed to shake the cream for hours in a closed glass bottle so the butter would form. With the rest of the milk, which was now a type of yoghurt, mom made fresh cheese—used for cheesecake—or my mother's special polenta. We liked fresh bread with butter and ham. Even Lola wanted some, but Dad told us to be careful because she was a dog and had a special diet. Moreover, Lola was his hunting dog, not a dolly.

I understood he was her boss, but he was not home all day long. We could still have Lola to ourselves for the majority of the day. This thought delighted me!

Someone knocked at the door, and when I opened it, I felt frozen. There was Daniel, the doctor, asking if my parents were home. I let him in the house, and a young lady followed after him.

"This is my wife, Mira," Daniel stated.

She said hello to me. She was tall and gorgeous with long, blond hair and black eyes.

Mom was watching and invited them to sit down. She called my father and introduced our guests, "George, this is my doctor and his wife. So nice of you to call on us." I knew she was not at ease.

"Glad to meet you. You must be Mr. Greg's son. You look so much like him," said Dad happily. He liked to meet intelligent people and enjoyed talking and spending time with them.

My sister, Lara, and I went out to play, as usual, when we had visitors. We heard laughing and pleasant talking from outside. When we went inside for water, we could see Daniel was in a room with Dad, and Mira was in another room with Mom— busy and chatting as if they had been friends forever. The men had sandwiches, cakes, and *the* bottle of brandy in front of them. The bottle I filled with water. My heart stopped for a second, and I ran into the kitchen. I was pouring water for Lara and me when Dad entered the room with the bottle in his hand. He was near me, looking directly into my eyes as he threw the bottle in the bin. He wore a smile, but his eyes were sending arrows.

"He knows!" I thought. I wanted to disappear in front of him. I jumped down and ran outside to Lara as I tried to forget everything. We played with our neighbours' children, and I ignored the black foreboding in my heart.

It was dark when Daniel and Mira left. From my neighbour's house, I saw their car leaving our yard. It was late, and we went back home. Dad seemed okay, and Mom was tidying the house and getting things ready for us.

Every night, before going to bed, we washed in a tub that Dad had improvised from a large basin. A watering can from the garden was our shower, and we enjoyed it. Half of the house and the bathroom were still under construction, but who cared? Our improvised shower was exciting.

I heard my parents talking about our guests, and their conversation was positive. Mira was a dentist, and Mom planned to take Lara and me for a visit. No problems. Or that is how it appeared at that moment.

The next day was fantastic! Lola stayed near me every step of the day. I read, and she sat next to me, pushing my hand from time to time to make me aware she wanted a cuddle. Her brown fur was soft, and she seemed made of chocolate. Lara was with her friends, playing somewhere. I had been reading all day long.

Dad came home with Daniel, set down his things from work, and they took off somewhere together. Now, this was strange. What did Daniel want? He inquired with Mom if had she managed the injections, and then he disappeared with my dad. I had the feeling something terrible was about to happen, but I forced myself to keep on reading.

Dad came back without Daniel, went inside the house, and started arguing with Mom. Daniel had told him to take care of her because she would need help to deal with her illness, and she did not need any stress. He was shouting at her that he was a good husband—doing everything he could to keep his family happy and healthy. I could not hear everything they were saying, but the gist of it was he did not like to be painted in a negative light.

I ran to play with my friends; I did not want to hear any more.

It was late when Lara and I returned home, and tension radiated through the air like electricity. They were still arguing, but now he was drunk as well. I knew this because he had *that voice*.

Then, he noticed my presence. "Take your bastard and go away!" His eyes were sending minacious arrows.

The word *bastard* hit me more than his voice. I had never heard that word, but it bothered me.

When delighted by Bachus' tricky potion1, Dad's voice was something that would make you run because you would feel like you were in danger.

---

[1]   In my culture, Bachus is the god of wine. If someone is drinking, they are said to be partaking in Bachus' potion.

Mom took me outside; we stopped on the stairs. I started to ask her about that word, but she changed the topic—asking me if I would like to go with Lara on a trip the next day. We could visit my grandfather and stay with my cousin Serena. I forgot everything else and felt happier. I wanted to jump up, rush inside, and tell my sister the excellent news. But I didn't.

Mom checked on my sister, who was sleeping. She came back outside, sat near me, and we talked for half an hour about the time she was a little girl and the places she played with her friends—on the hills around her village. Later we went to sleep, but I still thought about that word my father had said.

The next day, Dad was gone when we awoke. I found an old dictionary and looked up the word. *Did he mean I was an unpleasant person or that I was born of parents not married? Maybe they were not married? What was going on?*

Mom told us we were going to visit our cousin and our grandfather. We were thrilled about the two-hour trip on the bus. We had sandwiches and water, and someone would collect us when we arrived there.

Serena and her family gave us one week of happiness and joy. Every day, we went to see a new place. The hills around their village were full of fruit trees and bushes with berries. In the evening, we were all at my grandfather's home. We had to go through the cemetery to get there. Serena scared us, and we were running and laughing. Granddad awaited us with goodies and told us stories about his seven children.

We wanted to know more about Mom. But we were upset to learn his wife died when Mom was 12 years old. She was the oldest of the girls and started to take care of others. I could picture Mom doing this because she always took care of others, often forgetting about herself. I asked Granddad about my mother's wedding, and he showed me pictures. I was in peace with myself now. They were married. Hurray!

We missed our parents, and after one week we wanted to go home. Mom was so happy to see us. She had lots of goodies for

Lara and I, and when Dad returned from work, he had even more surprises. He kissed us both, and after dinner, he told us a new story about what happened when he was little. We loved these stories.

That night, I asked Mom what Daniel had said. Her face became gloomy, and her shoulders bent forward. Immediately, I wanted to take the question back, but now it was too late. She told me I needed to be careful what I said about Dad because he was a loving father and husband, and people would misunderstand me.

Sometime later, I found their wedding invitation and noticed I was born six months after the wedding.

"Is he my father?" I asked Mom.

"Oh, God, of course! You are his daughter, without a doubt. Look in the mirror; you and he have the same eyes and face. You have many similarities with him." And she kissed me.

Life started to get better once again.

My aunt Lila, from Bucharest, came for one week to stay with my granny. She had no children. We adored her. She looked like my father and was tall and beautiful with long, dark hair and smelled different from people I knew. She seemed like an actress from the movies.

Lola stayed near us, no matter what we were doing, and we were all happy again. Emotionally, the ominous clouds stayed far from us for days and sunshine enveloped us in warmth and joy.

Daniel was often going with my dad and his friends to fish and hunt; I could see how much he was growing to like Dad. Daniel brought lots of happiness to everyone, and Dad and his friends all loved him, heart and soul.

For the next two months, our home was filled with happy days. I was over the moon.

> "Have you ever been in love? Horrible, isn't it? It makes you so vulnerable. It opens your chest, and it opens up your heart, and it means that someone can get inside you and mess you up."
> Neil Gaiman, *The Kindly Ones*

CHAPTER 3

First Love

The first day of fifth grade, I started a new school in a nearby village. Students were attending from three small localities. I was very friendful, but there were lots of colleagues, new rules, new challenges, and four kilometres to walk to get to school in the morning and back in the afternoon. Physical exercise was my Achilles heel, but I knew walking would be good for my health. I wondered what would happen in the coming winter when it was -20 outside.

I noticed a charming girl, Amy, with blond hair and a cute hat, who I decided would be my friend. I introduce myself, "I am Daria. Nice to meet you. First-year?"

"Amy. Nice to meet you," she replied. She did not look at me, but I still felt we would be friends.

She had perfect, cured nails, so I hid my hands because they were ugly. I told myself I needed to change something if I did not want to be a country girl forever. I had never thought of curing my nails or even my bushy eyebrows. Mom told me that at 11, I was still a little girl, and I did not need to cure my eyebrows.

But she also never told me to have a look at my hands. I would show her when I got home. *Little girl.* At that moment, I felt a monkey from the forest. I was pretty, with my father's eyes and long hair, but I also looked like a monkey.

Amy became my best friend subsequently. After having a cat and dog as friends, I was happy to have a human friend. She was intelligent, and we competed at school. There were actually five of us—two girls and three boys—who were in constant competition for the entire four years at the school. We became advanced in almost all subjects, thriving on challenges—especially literature and math.

When the bell rang, we proceeded to our next class two by two. Lots of times while I was waiting in the row, I could see a handsome boy, on his own, outside the school wall. He had moles on his face, but they only enhanced his beauty. I found out he was a couple of years older than me. His name was Collin, and his parents were two of our teachers. I started to think of him more, even at home.

The fifth grade gave me contradicting feelings. I enjoyed most subjects. But I had two left hands when it came to sports—handball, running, volleyball, gymnastics. And I was also challenged by music. We had a gorgeous teacher, sophisticated and kind. Still, I did not understand the musical theory or the solfeggio (an exercise in singing using sol-fa syllables). Amy was perfect at sports and music, in fact, she played the pianoforte (a musical instrument like a piano). After many attempts, I gave up trying.

I had to accept myself how I was. I still wore two long braids, twisted back and tied behind my ears, with white bows—the way the Communist rule required.

I did not come in first place at school for the first year because of my grades in sports, but I did not care too much. I was good at the essential classes.

The teachers did not think the same, and every time they found me alone, I heard the same thing, "You are not good enough. Be more ambitious." Maybe the words were different, but the meaning was the same.

I became fed up with being told I was 'not good enough.' I was what I was. Even though I was not ambitious to learn certain subjects, I still had my interests. I hated sports, but I loved walking in the hills. I did not understand music theory, but I loved music—Tchaikovsky, Chopin, Brahms, Haydn, Vivaldi, Schubert, Liszt, Debussy, Verdi, Stravinsky, Mahler. I did not need to understand a solfeggio to enjoy music. Why could they not accept this?

Amy was a fantastic friend; I could tell her everything that popped into my head. She lived six kilometres from me, in a three-floor block of flats—the only one in that village.

The Communists, when they were in power, tried to regroup the population into flats, and the rumour was they were going to raze all the houses to make space for agricultural land. I worried about this because I loved my home. Still, it was exciting to visit her in her flat. She had a pianoforte in her living room, and she taught me a piece from "The Sound of Music:" do-re-mi-do-mi-do-mi-re-mi-fa-fa-mi-re-fa, etc. She played some songs for me, and I was a bit jealous. She told me our music teacher came to her house to teach her lessons. Now I understood why the teacher was always asking her to give the answers.

The sixth grade started with one month of farm work—picking potatoes. It was good because all the classes were together, working outside, so I could see Collin for hours. I had a bicycle, and he did as well, so we travelled to the farm in a group. Sometimes he teased me that I couldn't keep up with the group. I was over the moon at the attention. I did not care if I had to work eight hours in the hot sun, I was happy to be where he was.

Amy and I laughed as we started talking about how he moved, how he worked, and with whom he was chatting. Amy and I made a stew about every step he did.

Next year, he would attend high school in the city, and I worried about how I would see him.

Three colleagues (and competitors for our attention) found the notes Amy and I wrote during our lessons about my love. However, because we chose a girl's name for him, they were not sure who it was. Maybe they thought we meant them. After all, they were three perfectly good-looking boys. But my heart was all for Collin. I liked the idea of having an older boyfriend.

Yes, I was thinking of a boyfriend and Mom would be worried. I was only 13. Good thing she did not realized I noticed him when I was only 11.

I told Amy almost all of my secrets but not about my father's problem with brandy. Our fathers were friends, and I learned my lesson talking with Daniel. It was better to keep it to myself. I did not want to change what she thought about me.

We were chatting, most of the time, about my secret love for the teachers' boy, Collin. Though we knew he had a girlfriend, we tried to concoct something to be with him. Near the end of sixth grade, the whole school was invited to a year-end dance. Collin was responsible for the music, and I convinced Amy to go. But before I could go, I needed a cute dress. I did not have one, so I found something that suited me from my mother, and I told my parents we had a meeting at school. I could not have my hair styled because Mom would not have let me go, so I ended up going with my usual braids.

At the dance, Collin was with his girlfriend and his older brother—a university student. I heard the older boy asking who these gorgeous girls were, pointing with his eyes towards Amy and I. We could not hear Collin's answer. Still, after that, he kept watching us, even with his beauty in his arms.

The summer holidays after grade six were not happy for me. I kept thinking of my handsome guy. What was he doing, where was he spending time, and, moreover, who was he meeting with?

For the next two years, I did my best at school, but my situation remained the same in sports and music. My teachers kept telling me the same things:

- You are not ambitious enough.
- You need to be number one.

I suggested, to my colleagues, it would be nice to have dances at the school twice per month, and my dream became a reality shortly after. Collin supplied the music, so I could see him more often. I was glad his girlfriend was not with him. Someone told me they broke up over the previous summer. I could not be more delighted.

At the dances, he danced with a few girls, including Amy and I, but I could tell he preferred me. I melted in his arms when we danced. I dreamt of being his girlfriend, but I did not know how. Maybe it will come to be.

In the eighth grade, Amy told me she was going to move to the city. She would be my colleague for only one more month. I cried at home.

One week before she left, she put a note in my hand; I read it in class. I was concentrating so hard reading it, I did not see a colleague behind me reaching for it. He plucked the note from my hand. I was horrified when said colleague gave it to our head-master—a young, severe physics teacher. Many of us loved this teacher because he was closer to our age and was always helping us.

He read it and then gave it back to me. Smiling, he said, "It would be nice of you to answer; you have been friends for almost four years."

I stared at him, mute. I had seen only the first row, telling me we could not be friends anymore.

Picking up the letter, I continued reading. My heart began to pumping wildly, seeing what she had written. I kept a big secret (about my dad's drinking) from her, but she had a big secret too. She confessed her love for Collin, and because of this, she felt we could not be friends in the future. This upset me. I talked about him for more than three years, and she did not say a word. Though I could imagine her pain, I knew in my heart he liked me, not her. I felt sorry about that. She knew too; it was too much for her, so she wanted a fresh start—far from me, and from him.

Amy left. I was confused and hurt from losing her. I knew it was forever. Thankfully, I was lucky enough to be busy with school and preparation for high school. I passed the exams, and I was looking forward to seeing my sweetheart every morning. Amy attended another high school in the city, and I wondered why. That school was not to her standard; it was a simple high school. Yet she was so intelligent. She did not want to see me that much? My thoughts often went to her. At the same time, I could not change this situation.

September came and brought high school with it. In Romania, high school runs four years. Students' ages run from 14 to 18. Now I had to wake up at five in the morning to take the bus at six. The bus was always crowded. I tolerated it because this was the way for me to be near Collin. After catching the bus, I would go to the train station to meet Collin an hour before school. We then walked 20 minutes to the high school. Being around people forced us to restrain ourselves, and we wanted to be free to feel and touch each other.

Collin declared his love for me, and I was overjoyed. My first love. We now had four years full of new experiences ahead of us:

- The first time walking hand in hand;

- The first kiss;

- The dark cinema with lots of kisses for hours at a time;

- Time spent near the river, in the summer, hidden from curious eyes by bushes;

- Hours in the winter snow, on the nights when we could not stop caressing each other.

We never had sex, but the kisses never ended.

These four years were full of love and sadness because where passion finds a place, doubt and reality will sneak in soon enough.

He started to bring his family—his parents (my teachers), his big brother, and his little sister—to visit mine. Carla, his sister, was a small, sweet little girl, and I loved her. She was bright (as was all of the family) and fantastic company. Even Dad enjoyed it when she stayed with us, sometimes for days. I adored all of them, most of all, his father.

Collin and I had a kind of bond; I liked his irony. I think Dad was a bit overprotective, but it was not a problem. He respected Collin but mentioned to me that maybe Collin was not the right boy for me. I did not understand at that time what he meant. Later, Dad clarified with me that Collin was a very ambitious boy, and he would want someone more ambitious than me.

Was I not good enough again? Collin loved me.

Dad explained to me that maybe we were not rich enough for his ambition. He had the impression that Collin's parents felt more superior to my mom and him. *Because Mom was a housewife? She worked a lot, taking care of her family—but she had never been a dull hausfrau!* (A hausfrau is a housewife, in German.) I knew Collin loved Mom. He did not need to say it; I was aware of it. I was very proud of my parents because they were hard-working and intelligent people. They did not need to have a specific social position for me to be proud of them.

Collin and I found it hard to spend time privately together in the winter. The living room often had others in it—my sister, Mom, or Dad—and it was frustrating for us.

He complacently told me one week that all his family had visited a girl, Lisa, who was in the year below him at school. I knew she had a very convenient financial situation—with her father being an international driver.

"It was funny when we arrived. Lisa's mother was baking something, and the radio-cassette player on the table was full of flour. I helped her clean it, but she said it wasn't a big deal because they had plenty of these appliances in the house. Can you imagine? Some people can only dream of owning one, and some wouldn't be able to have one in their lifetime."

"Why did you visit them? And why did all the family go there?" I asked.

"We have a rule; we go everywhere together." But his answer did not satisfy my curiosity. It felt like there was a stone on my chest, and my father's words were buzzing in my head about how I was not ambitious enough for Collin. He was such an intelligent young man, yet so enthusiastic about this appliance.

As part of a younger generation, we were all wondering about the outside world. We lived under Communist rule, so only those who travelled abroad could had cool things. We could watch 'Dallas' on TV, but we could not believe how Americans lived. A TV remote was something from science fiction, for us, especially when we still had an old black and white TV box in 1986.

I liked all the things I could see in American movies, but I was happy with what I had. I never loved someone because of possessions or because of social standing. I was pleased to see new technology—and curious about it—but I was not jealous or willing to make friends because of what they possessed.

I no longer saw him in the same light; my disappointment was growing. On top of all this, I was frightened he would, one day, see my father drinking or witness a quarrel. Even though I saw something I did not like about him, I was in love with Collin, and all my thoughts were around him. I became depressed and did not concentrate on my courses. I excelled only in languages and literature, my favourites. Math, physics, and chemistry became a nightmare. Losing time thinking about Collin did not help me and was not a good reason for getting bad grades.

For the next two years, I attended the same high school Collin went to. He was at university, taking engineering. Being far apart did not help our relationship.

One of his friends took it upon himself to send me a poisoned arrow, saying, 'out of sight, out of mind.' (A poisoned arrow is something someone tells you to prevent you from something bad happening to you—in an indirect manner.) I supposed it was jealousy because his friend liked me, but the bell of doubt rang in my ears.

The summer after his first year at university, Collin told me he was going on a holiday to the Black Sea for two weeks with colleagues. I was so unhappy! At 16, I was still in high school. My parents will not let me go with him.

My new high school colleagues were different than those from my old school. Their expectations were lower. I could concentrate more on languages, but no one advised me to take this path.

My dream was to be a French teacher, but at the time, in Romania, this was frowned upon. As a young teacher, you had to go to a remote place for three years to gain experience, and after that, maybe, you could choose a school near your home.

During my second year of high school, I decided I would study economics at university—two years away. As a result, I had to continue in math, geography, and economic science—as preparation for the entrance exam. The problem was, I did not enjoy any of these subjects. I was too young to understand it would be better to follow my feelings and do a job I liked—instead of what others thought was suitable for me in our Communist society. The choice turned out to be a big mistake and a source of distress for the rest of my life, or until later, when I opened my eyes.

I was now 17 years old during my third year of high school. My new colleagues were all friendly, and I became friends with Ciel, a girl with big blue eyes and a velvety voice. She transuded calm and peace. Her presence made me happy—at ease. I was good friends with my desk mate, Sandra, who was energetic and always in a good mood; this helped with my depression and anxiety. We were chatting about our boyfriends, as girls usually do, but since Ciel did not have one, it was easier for me to talk to Sandra. She knew about the problems I had at home with my father, and she gave good advice on how to avoid bad situations and keep myself sane. Sandra did not take all the things in her life seriously but not because she was superficial. She developed a kind of system to defend herself against things that could hurt her soul. She would breeze through life like the wind, letting go, without thinking about what was terrible or gone from her life. She helped me live in the moment and enjoy life.

"I really don't see the point in getting upset over spilt milk," she used to say.

At school, we planned to go on a field trip to a mountain and Mom let me go. It was only 30 kilometres from my home, but it was the first time I was on my own without family around. We had a good time.

During the day, we wandered in the forest, walking for hours, without complaining or swimming in the lake to cool off. I loved nature and enjoyed hiking, even though I did not like sports class. In the evening, we got ready for a fire near the lake, and we had a barbecue. One of the boys played the guitar, and we all joined in singing. I had lots of time to chat with Ciel. We finished the trip inseparable.

Collin was a loving boyfriend, and our romance was as usual when he came home from university. I went to visit him, and he came to visit me—sometimes with all his family.

His mother became upset at the fact that my parents did not trust her enough to let me stay with them for a couple of days. My father informed me since Collin and I were not married, people in the village would talk. However, even when Collin was at university, my parents did not let me stay there overnight. I would have liked to have more time with Carla, Collin's sister. Instead, she was invited to stay with us for days at a time.

I was in my last year in high school, wrapping up studying. I got to thinking I would like to be in the same town as Collin, eventually—together—far from my parents' eyes.

I was looking forward to the Christmas holidays. We did not have cell phones, only letters to communicate. I knew I would see him on Christmas Eve. That day, groups of children sang carols, and we gave them cinnamon buns. After the children sang, much later on, teenage boys from the village came to sing. Lara, my sister, was a stunning girl and had several admirers. Therefore, we had lots of singers coming to the house. According to our custom, you needed to kiss one of the boys when they finished. I thought everyone wanted Lara's kiss.

I wore my best clothes to wait for Collin. I knew he would be late as he was coming from his village with his brother and some other boys. I waited for him until dawn. He did not appear. I was tired, and worried maybe he had some problems. Perhaps he would come during the day so he could stay longer with me.

My aunt and her new husband, a notorious footballer, were visiting my granny. My aunt asked me about my sweetheart, and I joked that he forgot me because he did not show up the previous night.

Days and nights flew by, yet he did not appear. I knew he was at home because a neighbour, who was his friend, told me. Maybe he finally decided I was not good enough for him.

My parents did not talk about him, but I saw them whispering and watching me when they thought I was busy with something. I tried to appear happy in front of them, but I cried every night when no one could see or hear me. I hated to see the pity in their eyes.

My school friends surrounded me for the Christmas holidays instead. I spent a lot of time with Ciel. I still wonder about how she listened to me quibbling on about my theories on what happened to Collin. She was a saint.

I played a happy girl in front of others for months after. No one knew I cried when I was alone. I knew Mom worried about me because she tried to talk to me about him, but I never accepted her offer. This upset her, and then she would sob while she let me in peace. I did not want her to feel sorry for me. Her health was failing of late because of her diabetes, and I did not want to stress her out more.

Without Mom knowing, one evening in the summer, I went to Collin's village—to attend a dance. His village was 3 km away. Collin was organising this soirée and providing the music. A friend asked me why Collin was not there keeping me under his loving wing; I told him we broke up. It was the first time I told someone this. It really hurt—my body and mind. I did not know what happened because Collin never contacted me. Instead, he disappeared from my life. I was not important enough, apparently, for him to give me an explanation. Before going home, my friend urged me to go to Collin and put my heart at peace.

I went to say hello to him. I do not remember all the details. Because it was night time, Collin walked me back to my village. Before entering my village, he said something about having a girlfriend, that things happen, and we kissed as before—for a long time. I went home in a trance, thinking he still loved me. It was good that my parents were not back from visiting their friends; they could not ask where I was.

Mom noticed I was over the moon the next day. She questioned me, and I told her about the previous night. It was a sweltering day, we were outside sitting on a pile of firewood.

"Did you know Collin's parents are visiting my friend, Ann? We were there last night at her farm. I have never seen so many pheasants in my life! They are breeding them and had hundreds. Collin's mother told Ann that he is in love with a colleague from the university. Her parents are also teachers—like them. Collin's mother feels this is a much suitable relationship for him and them." My mother related all of this to me.

I did not want to hear more. I could not describe my feelings at the moment—only pain in my heart. "Let's not talk any more about it. Let them be happy with their new in-laws. Teachers!" The words fell from my mouth in a jumble; my eyes were cast downward, watching the ground.

"I am so sorry, Daria! I would never think or want to hurt you. I liked him, and I am disappointed in his choice. It is better to let him go. He does not love you as you do him."

"Don't worry, Mom, I love you. You're right, I should move on." With that said, I informed Mom I had a headache and went inside.

I went into a room in the front of the house, where I remained all day long in the company of my miserable feelings.

Mom and Dad were going to the river. Lara was somewhere with friends. I decided to write two long letters—one for Mom and one for Collin. I do not remember the words I wrote.

Calmly, I located the keys for my father's 'secret' place, where he kept the hunting rifle. However, I was not interested in the gun. He kept some strychnine candies there for animals. There were 7 or 8 candies; I took one. After locking the safety deposit box, with my hand on the doorknob, I re-thought and went back for another one.

Back in the room, I closed the letters, put names on them, and went to my bed with the candies and a glass of water. I swallowed the candies, then I put my head on the pillow and fell asleep.

In the middle of the night, I opened my eyes to the inviting smell of cooked fish. I could hear my parents laughing. I remembered what I did. I saw the letters on the table. My body was shaking as I burned the letters.

I was in hell for weeks but had no pain or other signs I would die. Maybe I was not even good enough for the worst place I could imagine—hell. I realised my father could have gotten into a lot of trouble and went to prison for malpractice with hazardous substances. It would have been my fault—on top of the pain he would have experienced if he had lost a daughter. Now I knew I wanted to live and make them happy. They did not deserve all of this because of my stupid love for an obtuse boy. I loved life, and I decided I would never do this again.

I did not pass the entrance exam at university, and neither did Ciel. We were miserable, but together we could fight off the feeling of being losers.

Her father found her a job in a place full of gypsies. She was humiliated working with the gypsies but did her job.

Mine did not send me to work, he sent me far from home—12 hours away by train—and made me study. The next year, I passed the exam.

My next stop was Bucharest—where Ciel now lived. She had a huge surprise in store for me!

"You can never know exactly what another person is thinking…And, the worst part it's…They are usually not thinking about you at all."
Portia Nelson, *The Romance of Self-Discovery*

CHAPTER 4

The Big City

Ciel was now a student at the Drama and Film Academy, and I was extremely proud of her. People tried for years to attend this Academy, but only a few people passed the hard exam. Hurray! Yes, she would do theatre, and I would do bloody economics. At least one of us would be living our dream.

Ciel and I were free, in the capital of Romania. There were around 20 theatres, cinemas, operas, and hundreds of places to spend time. It was a new world for us.

My parents were on their own now as my sister was in high school, living as an intern. She went home on the weekends but on the weekdays, they were alone.

It was tough for me to go far from Mom. When I took the bus to school, she was there, outside the house, waiting for me. I remember her leaning against the fence and waving to me. I could sense her sadness from the bus. Knowing she had health complications and was working too much, did not help my worries.

Dad was a bit hard on her; he liked to offend her, calling her 'the diabetic' when he was on the side of Bacchus. I saw her eyes, covered by a shadow of sadness. She loved this man with all her heart, regardless of how he treated her.

I wanted to be independent, to have money to send her on a fantastic holiday. My parents went on a one week holiday some years prior—to the Black Sea. This was their one and only holiday together during their entire life. They were always busy and never had time for any other holidays.

Bucharest was too chaotic and big for my taste. People were always in a hurry, and they smiled with irony when hearing me speak. I was a girl coming from a small village. My accent was different from the people of Bucharest. Their eyes seemed to tell me I was not good enough for them, because of me being provincial. They were posh; I was nothing. This only happened in shops around the city; at university, it was another story. My colleagues were friendly; my place of birth was not an issue.

I found a place to live, in a dorm with mixed students. The small dorm room I was to live in had four beds and a wardrobe. Three other female colleagues shared this space with me. It was not the ideal place to live; I did not like it. The dorm was noisy, and you had no privacy. Sometimes someone was crazy enough to bring a boyfriend into their bed for the night. It felt uncomfortable, but I tried to keep my feelings to myself. One did not want to be branded a 'provincial.' A provincial was someone who came from a small, rural area.

I had always shared a room with my sister. But I loved her, and it was different. Now, I dreamt of a place only for me.

For the first year of university, I continued to live in the dorm. During my second year of university, my cousin Chloe and I moved into an old house together—near the university. Her father, a colonel in the army, had a friend in Bucharest who owned a house. We were lucky to have this opportunity and happy to live together.

Chloe, a student in nuclear physics, understood physics, mathematics, and chemistry. She was unique in her own way. She must have had a higher IQ than most people. She could talk about lots of topics, and everyone considered her a living encyclopedia. I was very proud of her. She was beautiful, resourceful, and bright. She knew her value but had problems related to men. She would start a relationship, and shortly after, her boyfriend would be overwhelmed by her knowledge and step away. She did not know how to dumb herself down—fakely or playfully—and let them feel superior if they were not. Chloe and I talked a lot about boys. We would have liked to have relationships. She felt there was something wrong with her because she did not feel loved, and the boys would all disappear. I advised her to listen more when the boy wanted to show off, but she could not. It was beyond her comprehension why she should have to.

I had problems too. I was still thinking of Collin, and I did not like this university. I was taking economics—something I didn't like. I wanted to be a French teacher, not an accountant! I made a big mistake in my career path. I wanted to change majors and study languages. Still, I continued down my chosen path and continued to hurt myself by staying the course. I discovered I could be truant a lot. You were not forced to attend all the classes if you could secure the study material from a colleague. These rules changed before I started my first year at university when the country experienced a revolution, and we got the Communists out of the way.

During my first year of university, I went to a posh party with some students studying medicine. There were lots of foreigners; I heard Greek, Syrian, English, and French languages being spoken. I understood only the French conversations, in fact, I partook in one with a group of girls, who were amazed at how well I managed the Moliere language.

I wandered around the house—in and out of various rooms—until I found a sophisticated ice cream machine in front of me.

"You look like Alice in Wonderland. What is so interesting about this box? Have one. I am Paul, by the way." A handsome guy was near me. He had a strange accent but spoke my language perfectly. I did not—could not—tell him I had never seen such a modern ice cream machine. He gave me some ice cream, and we found ourselves talking for hours.

Paul was from Switzerland. His mother was from my country but with German origins. He was attending his last year of medicine and would then go back to Geneva to learn brain surgery. During the night, someone mentioned to me I was lucky to be noticed by him because "he had a title too." I smiled because 'the title' didn't mean anything to me. Collin would have been thrilled to meet someone posh, but for me, it was all rubbish. Paul was a pleasant surprise because he was not pompous and never showed off. It was easy to talk to him, and he did not seem to be aware of how handsome he was. I thought he had chosen an outstanding education and, maybe, he felt sorry for me. I was not very happy at the time, and I never saw myself as an interesting or beautiful girl.

"Don't bother with all these people; you are not good enough for them!" I was thinking. I fully expected to never see Paul again.

Two weeks later, we met near my school. Paul invited me to eat, and after we were going to the cinema. He kissed me, and I liked it, but it was different than it was with Collin. I did not feel butterflies in my stomach. My body was near him, but I felt empty of feelings and far away. He was patient and calm, and I seemed to have a kind of mysterious power over him, making this sophisticated boy appear as my slave.

We saw each other only on weekends because he was busy. Paul had surprises for me every time we met. I wanted to talk to Ciel about him, but it was impossible to find a moment in her busy school schedule. I knew he loved me, and he kept trying to fix me—to heal my pain. Despite everything he did or said, I felt nothing like a girlfriend should feel. It seemed I was not in the mood to fall in love.

I went home for the winter holidays, and I noticed my mom was poorly. My sister went out dancing with friends one night when my father had visitors to the house. He asked Mom to cook something. She was so sick—vomiting—she could not leave the bed. He made a fed-up grimace and babbled something unkind about her situation.

I would have liked to be strong enough to slap his perfect face and make him sober for a minute. I glared at him.

"Don't look at me like that! I hate what I see in your eyes. Who do you think you are? And tell the missus it would be nice for her to cook something. She is always sleeping," he shouted at me.

"I will cook something, be patient," I told him, trying to keep calm, but I was worried more about Mom than him having food for his visitors.

The next day, we had to call an ambulance for Mom; she would never come back. I visited her in the hospital for a week, and her situation was not good. I had to back to school within a couple days for my first exam at university. Mom told me to stay calm because she would be fine. I was happy she was in the hospital and not at home. I thought she would sleep a bit, and no one would be mad at her.

The last day at home, it was icy and snowing heavily. The temperature was -20 degrees, and the bus did not come. I stood outside on the road for two hours, but I could not find transport to get to the hospital.

I returned to school with a broken heart. I could not see Mom before leaving, and it was frustrating.

Once in Bucharest, I started studying. I told Chloe about Mom. She was unhappy as well. The days passed. The night before my first exam, my aunt called. I knew her call was about Mom. Sure enough, Mom had died in the hospital.

I became dead inside. I cannot describe my feelings. There was pain all over my body, and I could not talk. I just continued, calmly, to watch the film on TV—the one I was watching before the call. I did not register anything, and I did not want to speak to Chloe. She called another cousin, who came to see me.

During the 20-hour train ride home, I thought of nothing. This feeling remained once I got back. Sometimes this feeling accompanies me even today, after 29 years.

Without Mom—the heart of our home—it was merely a house, nothing more. Going 'home' after Mom's death—for years after—was painful. I could see Mom in every tree in the garden and in every piece of furniture. The first time home after Mom's death, I could not look my father in the eyes because I was frightened we would argue. I knew it was hard for him too, but I hated him right then.

"He pushed her into that grave!" I spewed with all of the hate I was capable of, to Granny.

"You all pushed her there! Did you or your sister help her?" Granny responded, crying. She loved Mom.

I cried for months after when no one could hear or see me. *Who can understand what is in your heart?*

Paul was more than perfect, and was ready to give me the moon if only he could see a smile on my face. He took me to Switzerland for a week. We flew there. The house was near Lac Lemon. Only his mother was at their home.

Before we left, his mother approached me and told me to break it off with Paul if I did not love him. She saw how cold I was with him. Though she was very polite, the message was clear.

Once in Bucharest, I told him about my feelings. I adored him, but not in the way he deserved. He told me to contact him with any problems I might have in the future. I broke his heart, and he still cared for me.

Paul returned to Switzerland.

I knew I was stupid for letting him go, but I stayed the course with my decision. *Was I a masochist who entered only relationships where love was shown in the form of fighting, drama, tears, doubt, and insecurities?* With Paul, this was not the case—he treated me perfectly. He did not play with me, and I felt his love. And yet, I could not reciprocate it. *"Yes,"* I concluded, *"I must be crazy."*

Summer came, and I went to the Black Sea with Ciel; it was our first universitarian holiday. Every day, we sunbathed—taking breaks only for meals. We spent our nights dancing, and we made friends. We did not look for boyfriends because we knew boys there were only looking to enjoy themselves for a short time. Nothing serious would come of any 'relationships' that happened there. I did not want to be used for sex only, and I needed time to grow within a relationship before I would have sex. Chloe and I were inexperienced in love, and, at 21, we were both still virgins.

After a few days under the sun, we needed to do something else, so we went to the students' club for an hour of tennis or badminton in a cooler place, temperature wise. However, they only had a chessboard and pieces to play. We found a place to play it.

From a nearby table, two very looking guys were laughing and watching us. Maybe they thought we were some super-intelligent girls preferring chess to the sea or boys. We chatted with them a bit and decided to meet up again that night.

Their names were Alan, who seemed to prefer me, and Gabriel, who liked Ciel. We were happy with this; they were both lovely. Alan as very tall, almost two meters, and I felt tiny and insignificant near him. Especially when I was not wearing high heels. I did not understand why he was spending time with me. Every step he took, girls were watching him, and I knew he was the kind of man who could have whomever he wanted. I was pleased to be near a man like him—and envied by other girls.

The next day, the boys took us with them to sunbath at their place. We met their friends, but not even one of the girls was happy to see us. I was pleased that Alan spent his attention only on me; everything was perfect.

The second night, after dancing, the boys suggested a midnight swim in the sea. It sounded exciting. But they were naked, and we were not comfortable doing the same. We did not watch them until they were far away in the water, and we kept our nickers on.

Alan waited for me to swim out to him; keeping a bit of distance from Ciel and Gaby. He caressed me and laughed when he put his hands on my back and felt my nickers.

"Hahaha!" He laughed. "How old are you? Are you still a virgin? Oh, God!" He continued to kiss me while he was teasing me.

Sometime later, we got out of the water, put our clothes on, and directed them to the hotel. Gaby was laughing, and I heard him tell Alan how 'lucky' they were to both find a virgin. He noticed my trousers were wet around the crotch area and had a laugh about this.

I was not expecting to see them the next day, but they were both after us. Alan was taking care of me, as usual, but, at the dance later, I noticed him talking with a girl —even disappearing into the crowd for a moment. Too long a moment for my liking.

A French boy came over and invited me to dance. He told me I looked like a very distinct and elegant girl from Paris.

Alan found me after, and it was clear he did not like me dancing with someone else. It bruised his ego.

Before leaving our vacation, Alan and I exchanged phone numbers, and we agreed to meet in September.

I needed to go home, to see my father and determine how he was coping without Mom. After my mother died, he used to call me in the morning, and I was always happy to hear his voice. I loved him—and I hated him—depending on the memories I had at the moment. When I remembered him careful and sober, I loved him. When I remembered him drunk, I hated him.

I told Chloe everything about the holiday; she was thrilled and curious about Alan.

While I was gone, a colleague of mine started to visit Chloe, and I knew they liked each other. I was looking forward to September to see how our romances turned out.

Collin was marrying this summer. My aunt invited me to visit her. I think Granny talked to her and asked my aunt to keep me busy. I was not suffering from the news of his marriage. I was happy to put a stone on everything with Collin's name on it.

One of my cousins took me to the airport, where he had friends working as pilots. I had a great time with these boys, flying over top of the city when they were doing their training hours.

My aunt had excellent connections. Her husband was now the big boss of a national club. As a result, I often talked on the phone to people from television or known personalities when they called my aunt and uncle's home. They had guests every day, and I kept busy and stayed happy.

I wanted the summer holidays to end, not because I was bored, but because I wanted to meet Alan again.

My father was not well. He played the happy man, but I could hear him during nights, talking in his sleep. I knew he was talking with Granny. He was taking care of the house, but she was doing too much work. We loved her, but we did not want to be bossed around by her. We felt like we were enrolled in the army. From the morning to the evening, she found lots of jobs for us around the house: picking fruits for hours, digging, retrieving the hay or wheat crop, milking the cows.

One day, when Lara and I were picking plums in the garden, a visitor came for my sister. A good-looking boy from the city. Granny told him he could stay to talk to Lara only if he worked with us. I had never seen Lara so upset. The guy never came back to see her again.

In September, I went back to the capital. I had a date with Alan at his home. Chloe told me to wear the best lingerie I had because it was clear why he was inviting me there. I put on the best clothes I had went to Alan's home. Gaby was there when I arrived. We watched a film, and after Gaby left, Alan wanted me to stay the night. I was ready. It was an interesting night, and I wondered if girls talked about sex. It was not as romantic as it appeared in films. I felt guilty after—my provincial education was showing. I thought I did not know Alan well enough. He was perfect and loving, but in my head, a warning bell was sounding. I missed Paul, but I did not want to think about him.

On the Tube, I had more time to think, and I asked myself what was in my mind when I chose a man. I was in love with this stranger, and I knew in my bones it was the wrong choice.

For one year, it was a strange relationship with Alan. Sometimes I felt loved. He would take me to dance and meet his friends. In the winter, we went skiing, and he was kind, teaching me for hours how to put the boots on, how to steer with my legs, and how to move down the hill. But sometimes I thought he wanted to see me for one reason.

Gaby had a girlfriend, so I had company when the boys were busy playing Bridge.

I met Alan's parents. They were fascinating, but we do not see them a lot.

I liked his parents, but I was busy attending courses at university, studying, and spending time with friends.

My best friend at university was Mary. She was always happy and had lots of friends. She was intelligent, beautiful, hardworking, and earnest. Her fiancé was her sweetheart from her village, and she never cheated on him. She believed they would marry, and her heart belonged to him. I adored her. We studied, cooked, and ate together. Even though we made other girlfriends, we spend a lot of time together.

A male colleague, who visited Chloe wanted to talk to me about her. He liked her, but she always wanted to have the last word, and he was becoming overwhelmed. He was speechless around her. I understood what he meant. She did not know to let a man win. She knew everything about everything, and she believed you knew nothing compared to her. She did not do it on purpose. I always wanted to be as bright as her. Still, I understood men had difficulties being with a woman who was too intelligent. It was too much for them, and they felt worthless. I could not help him because I tried to tell her this in the past. She would never change or play a 'dolly' to keep a man. I let them solve their own problems.

That summer, Alan wanted to go together on holiday, to the Black Sea coast. We went to Mamaia, a small town near Constanta, that had a super long, stunning beach. We went with Gaby and his girlfriend. For one week we happily enjoyed the blue water and the sun. On the beach, girls were watching Alan, and some even had the audacity to put a note with their phone number in his hand. He looked as if he was not interested when this happened, but later I saw him copying the numbers into his notebook.

Alan was often miserable, and his mother told me he loved a woman who broke his heart. Since then, he was never the same. I tried to 'fix' him for a year, thinking my love would change him, but it made no difference. He was a beautiful person, but while he liked me, I was not 'the one' to make his heart jump or give him butterflies in the stomach. My situation with Paul was now reversed.

The last night on our holiday, we went for a long walk and talked. He told me he felt unhappy. Even his friends told him he looked depressed. Maybe, he said, he needed to meet other girls. One day, he might meet someone who made him happier.

I let him go, but I was so dreary all night that I could not talk. There was only emptiness inside.

Back in Bucharest, I felt lonely. I stayed there for two days on my own, then I went home for the other two months of summer. Chloe was at her parents, too. The words 'not good enough' swirled in my brain. I thought, at that moment, I was not tall enough, not intelligent enough, not lovable enough, and not sparkling enough.

I remembered when I went to my cousin's wedding with Alan, and he said to me he wanted me to be like my aunt. She was a noticeable woman; modern and sophisticated. Even the bride's cousin noted I was lovely. Then added it was a pity I was not taller. Remembering all this made me miserable.

I bought a train ticket. The voyage was 12 hours long. I had two stunning boys as a company in the carriage. I did not sleep all night on the train because these boys, brothers, fought all night between them, trying to make me give them my number phone and convince me to have a date with one of them. I was pleased with their attention but not in the mood to have a rendezvous.

At home with Lara and Diana, the neighbour's granddaughter, I remained for a few weeks. Diana was living with us most of the time and felt like a new sister. Lara and Diana had friends and went out often to dance or to take in the theatre; at least they were able to enjoy themselves. I was still in a foul mood about Alan.

My aunt invited me to stay with her for some time, so I did. However, Alan still worked for her. He was looking for a job some months before, and I convinced my uncle to hire him. I wanted to help Alan, hoping he would love me more for this. I was pitiful. My cousin teased me a lot. We talked about Alan, what he was doing at work, and who was dating. Not that I wanted to, but my cousin seemed to enjoy hurting me.

My aunt was sweet, taking me on trips and involving me with her cheerful friends. She wanted me to smile again.

For the rest of the holiday, I met up with Ciel, read books or went to the river to fish or swim.

I helped Dad with the gardening, especially with the flowers. We argued a lot, and one day, when I was helping him in the garden, suggesting new items to add to it, he told me I had expensive ideas. Apparently, he did not understand why I was so different from the rest of our family. I recalled the word 'bastard,' and I became upset. *He still thought maybe I was not his daughter?* I left him digging on his own, upset he did not want to embrace some of my ideas on planting new flowers. From the yard, he could not be seen because of the roses growing all around the fence. I walked toward the main gate.

A man entered the gate. "Hello! It is your father at home?" he asked.

"I don't know who you are talking about. I live across the road." I answered in a bad mood.

"I'd have sworn you were George's daughter; you look just like him," he continued.

"Sorry, but you are wrong. My father is 'X,' and we live on the opposite…"

"She is my daughter, Peter. Let her in peace; she is only joking!" Dad interrupted from behind the rose bushes.

Now I felt so happy. If I looked like my dad to this person, I could not have another father.

The next day, taking the bus to Ciel's village, a man I had never seen before, asked me if I was George's daughter. He knew Dad because of his work as a vet—another confirmation I was my father's daughter. Since he was from Ciel's village, he invited her and me to visit him. He treated us with cherries and sent some back with me for my father. I remembered how people loved Dad, and I was proud.

The last three years at university flew by.

Alan went to Korea for a year to work as an engineer, and we saw each other again when he came back. We had broken up but decided to start our relationship again. He wanted to move to America and asked me to go with him. I could not understand it. I decided I would break up with him after a holiday in France; one we planned to go on together. I wanted to have the last two weeks of summer with him, and then I ended the relationship for good.

I even decided to move home. My sister needed to rest a bit after all these years of taking care of our father; she had done it for five years now.

I told Ciel all about my feelings. She saw me on holiday when she was visiting her family.

Chloe would be another two years at university, in the capital, to complete a Master's in nuclear physic and work in an institute.

Alan moved to America, and I went home. I could not picture myself with him, so far from home. I was frightened one day he would meet the love of his life, but I would remain alone all my life.

I looked for a job in a nearby city. At home, I started to dust and clean. My father had taken to carving in his room, and it was a mess. He was sober now and even cooked. He never prepared food before. I felt sorry for him, in a way, but I am glad he was in a good state of mind.

A guy came to see Dad, and we spent some time together. He made me laugh. I had never seen someone laugh like him; he was so funny. His name was Oliver; he asked me if I wanted to meet again.

When Dad came home, I told him about Oliver. He started laughing.

"Be careful, my dear. I know Oliver is married, and I do not want problems with his father, my friend. Oliver has a daughter and a beautiful wife. Though I think he is a bit strange," said Dad.

Not the news I was expecting. I liked Oliver, but he had not said a word about his family. Of course, there was something wrong with him; I was attracted to problematic men. This was certain. I knew it by then.

When Oliver came again, I asked him about his family. I still cannot remember how he convinced me to start a relationship with him. He kept coming, and we would go fishing or wandering in places I had never been to. Eventually, we found ourselves falling in love, and we could not stop.

One day he found out his wife had an affair with a man he knew. All his friends already knew about it, and his ego was damaged. He had told me before this that his marriage was a mess. His wife was pregnant at 18, and they were forced to marry—by their parents. He felt trapped by a wife when he was only a boy, and they both were unhappy now. I wondered if he considered it ironic his wife found another man. After all, he was with another woman—me.

Oliver lived in a flat with his parents, wife, and daughter. I could not understand this. His parents were sweet, but they had their own house near the city. Oliver and his wife could have moved there and lived on their own. He had degenerate arguments with his wife. They were arguing all the time, and the situation was getting worse and worse. She and her daughter moved to a new flat. Finally, separation would set them apart.

I expected him to feel free, but it was worse than ever. His daughter told him about her mother's boyfriend, and it was all Oliver could talk about. I thought he was jealous because she left him for a professional. Moreover, his wife's new boyfriend's wife called Oliver to talk about the situation and what they needed to do. They spoke for hours.

I told Oliver's mother it was insane, and I would break up with her crazy son. She assured me he was better off without her and that this worry would pass.

Oliver pushed me to apply for a job near my house, and I secured my first place of work after university. I was an accountant, and I had an office. All-day long, I revised bills and worked on salaries. I started to wonder if I would feel gratified doing this for the rest of my life. This was it? I would wait for holidays once a year and work like a donkey for the rest of the time. It was so dull! I was sure about one thing, I did not enjoy this type of work.

I became pregnant. Oliver and I talked. He did not tell me what to do outright but started to brainwash me, reminding me of his unhappiness when he was forced to marry his first wife. He told me he never had the opportunity to choose when to have a wife and a child. And he reminded me how hard his life was already.

Listening to him, I asked myself why I was still with him. However, I could not find the courage to tell him what I was thinking this to his face. I did not want to have this tie to him. I saw how he liked to boss around women near him, how he wanted to have the final word, and how he thought he knew everything. I started to understand why his ex wanted fresh air.

I had an abortion. Oliver was so gentle, taking care of me, and playing the perfect partner. Our parents did not know about it, and I wanted to keep it in this way.

I felt guilty about all this, and I had horrible dreams. New ones that added to my other nightmares from my childhood.

Oliver's wife had a big row with her new boyfriend and wanted to try again with her husband. During that time, people didn't really get divorced. Even if they were separated, they were still considered married. Maybe it was right for him to try to work things out, especially since there was a child involved. So, I told him he must try it. It was not that I was happy to let him go. I explained my feelings to him—that he would never be satisfied with her and he was wasting his time. He was upset and told me he understood why I said this, but after all, I should have known what was doing with him was wrong—knowing he was married. He was cruel, but I took it! Point for him.

Diana, my sister's best friend, got married in Italy to a gorgeous man. Lara also got married—in Italy as well. I was happy for them both.

My brother-in-law was the best thing that ever happened to my sister, and I knew they would be perfect together.

Diana had a one-year-old daughter, and now Lara gave me a niece, Lydia. The day my niece was born, my father and I were crying like children. I wanted to be with her.

Lara sent me money for a visa and wanted me to come to Italy. All I wanted was to go far from all my failures.

My boss at work tried to caress my legs when I was sitting near him, and I knew my time at this company was at an end. I pushed his hand away, and he did not like it.

I went to get a visa, but the money was not enough. I had to buy travel insurance, due to new rules, which was very expensive. What money I had was not enough for the train ticket to get back home. And there was no extra for a coffee or a sandwich. It was frustrating and shameful. I bought a ticket for a bit more than halfway, and I prayed to God for Him to help me. I was lucky, but now I had a considerable headache.

At home, there was another surprise. My father was drunk again and forgot the coffee on top of the cooker that morning. There was an explosion. No more glass remained in the windows, and from the kitchen, I could see the sky through a hole in the roof. Moreover, the police were there because Dad had accused me of wanting to kill him. Luckily, I was in another place at the time.

The police, unfortunately, knew my father. Even though they liked him, they understood the situation and were sorry for all the hassle. Everyone knew my father was a kind of Dr. Jekyll and Mr. Hyde, with both a good and an evil side.

I was not working anymore; I had left the job as an accountant in Romania to travel to Italy. I needed money, again, from Lara. She never complained when the home was involved. She loved the house and Dad. Before I left for Italy, the house was like new—even better than before the explosion.

Just before I left, an old colleague from work, Mrs. S, called me and asked about Oliver. I told her we were no longer together. I guess he tried to visit me at work, but no one knew anything about him.

"He never should have come to the place you worked. It was disrespectful toward you. We all love you so much," she told me.

I did not understand what she was talking about or why he had gone there.

"I didn't know about a wife." She explained that he had come to her and asked her for a loan. He told her he had to pay for his wife's debts. Mrs. S was disappointed with him.

He must have been desperate. I could not meet with him and ask him what was happening. I was sorry he had problems. I knew him though, and I believed whatever he was doing, it was for his daughter and his parents. They were all lovely and did not deserve trouble.

During the trip, I smiled when thinking of Lydia. I tried to imagine her and what it would feel like with her in my arms.

I was sorry Dad would be lonely. What would happen to him while I was gone? Maybe he would find someone to be with.

"I like the night. Without the dark, we'd never see the stars."
Stephenie Meyer, *Twilight*

CHAPTER 5

New Life

Within Lydia, a new life was blooming in our family. I had the ticket for the coach; the luggage was ready. I wanted to see Italy and my three-month-old niece.

I was still thinking a lot about Oliver. I did not understand myself. Somehow, I knew we would be together again. Stupidity, I knew, but I was a masochist who enjoyed hurting herself as much as possible. In all the unhappiness I put myself through, I found something exciting that pushed me forward. I wanted to make Oliver happy and have a quiet life together. Poor me! I had a big problem: my brain was processing wrong. I knew it, yet I continued with the same thoughts.

Travelling on the coach was exhausting, and my legs swelled. My curiosity about Italy grew. We arrived at the checkpoint. The customs officers were young, handsome, and very well-groomed. They checked us, and I had the feeling they despised us. I heard them talking about us. I understand the words 'bloody Romanians.'

I forgot about those two words once when we were in Florence. I was passing near Duomo—a cathedral. I told myself that one day, I would return here to see Giotto and Brunelleschi's work with my own eyes. I wanted to see the Uffizi Gallery (art gallery), Palazzo Vecchio (museum), Piazza della Signoria (L shaped square in front of Palazzo Vecchio). I could see Ponte Vecchio (arched bridge) from a distance, and I was overjoyed.

The next stop was Rome, and then we were in front of the Forum and the Colosseum. I saw busy people walking near these beauties, with their indifference of witnessing the same sights every day. I was amazed by the ancient Romans' knowledge of building something that could withstand time and be seen after 2,000 years.

Two hours later, we were in Abruzzo. This town's name reminded me of a film, "A Farewell to Arms," 1957, with Rock Hudson, Jennifer Jones, and Vittorio De Sica—based on Hemingway's book. De Sica played the priest, and he described his birthplace, Abruzzi, to the Americans. His voice, and the beauty he was describing made me curious at the time. So, I promised myself I would visit Abruzzo one day. Here I was!

The coach left us in a city on a hill where I could see the sea. The view took my breath away.

My brother-in-law, Alessandro, drove me to their home. With Lydia, it was love at first sight. She was a healthy child and had wonderful parents. Alessandro was the best father she could have. He was always happy and kind to everybody. I never heard him gossiping about people. He liked hearing us women chatting. If he found something funny in what we said, he laughed without giving an opinion. He was the kind of man who saw something good in everyone.

I loved being with Lara and Lydia, but I needed to work to start a proper life in this new ambient country, Italy. I was doing lots of odd jobs because it was hard to be a carer or a shop-girl after being an accountant. I learned the language properly, but I still could not find a suitable job.

I spent all my free time with my little niece. I was lucky that my sister was not a jealous mother.

The sea was three kilometres from the town, and I enjoyed walking on the long beaches. When Lydia started to walk, I took her to the beach.

She was chubby, sweet, and wore a big smile on her face as her father did. I adored her!

Her first day on the beach, she made me laugh. Lydia was good at walking around the house, but the sand was more challenging. She tried to keep on her feet but fell each time. I took a book with me, and though I would have liked to read, she kept calling me, wanting attention.

Near us, a girl and two boys were playing in the water are. They were only four or five years old. Lydia watched and called out, "Hey, children, come here!"

I wondered how she was not too shy to talk with people she did not know. I was trying to read—with the eyes in my book—but I still heard her.

"Hello, I am Lydia. Go and bring me some water," she told the other children as she gave them two little buckets. The children brought her water three or four times and were talking to her. She was the smallest among them, but she had the presence like she was their captain.

"Mmm," I thought, *"what a commander my little roly-poly is."*

I helped her go into the water, where she played with her new friends. At 8 pm, she was still playing, and it was hard to convince her to come home.

"Lydia, it's time to go home. We must be on time for the bus." I tried to convince her.

"No! I like the water. If you don't let me in peace, I will shout something bad…a word you don't like…"

We stayed there for one more hour because I did not want to take the risk. It was not so easy with children. I asked myself how mothers of two or three managed these situations.

I saw Lydia was very independent, and she was not shy to say what she felt. She was only three years old, yet she amazed me with her strong character. When I was a little girl, if my parents told me to do something, I always did what they asked, without commenting.

Lydia remembered Chloe—my cousin. Chloe used to talk about everything with her parents, even things they did not like or approve of. Lydia was the same. She was not frightened.

I had many rules as a child. Rules about how to conduct myself at the table, how to talk to my parents, how not to talk to strangers, responding to requests—even how to walk, sit, and sleep. I was cautious about pleasing my family; if I liked something my family did not like, I gave up my choice. Later in my life, at university, I had new rules to follow. My aunt, Mara, became like my boss—because she was paying for all my needs for years two, three, and four. (My father paid my first year's fees, and I paid my own way for the fifth year.) I was frightened to say what I really thought about things; I would tell her what she liked to hear.

Needless to say, given my upbringing, I was amazed at how a three-year-old girl could be so independent.

Oliver was trying to get in contact with me again. After one year with his wife, trying to keep his family together, he was a free man once more. Things did not work between them.

I knew this would happen. I started to dream about a life together.

For a year, we talked on the phone, and now he was ready to come to me, in Italy. The only problem which remained was to find him a work contract for a visa. He was working in a bank, and it would be hard for him to take a lower-paying, simple job.

I felt it was all a mistake, but I could not stop myself. I remembered Portia Nelson and her *Autobiography in Five Short Chapters*—a story I loved.

Chapter I

I walk down the street.
There is a deep hole in the sidewalk.
I fall in.
I am lost...I am helpless.
It isn't my fault.
It takes me forever to find a way out.

Chapter II

I walk down the same street.
There is a deep hole in the sidewalk.
I pretend I don't see it.
I fall in again.
I can't believe I am in the same place.
But it isn't my fault.
It still takes a long time to get out.

Chapter III

I walk down the same street.
There is a deep hole in the sidewalk.
I see it is there.
I still fall in...it's a habit.
My eyes are open.
I know where I am.
It is my fault.
I get out immediately.

Chapter IV

I walk down the same street.
There is a deep hole in the sidewalk.
I walk around it.

Chapter V

I walk down another street.
Source: https://en.wikipedia.org/wiki/Portia_Nelson.

I came to Italy for a fresh start, and here I was wanting my past boyfriend with me. Alessandro tried for three years to find me a nice boyfriend, but I did not like anyone. Eventually, he and Lara let me do what I wanted, so they could see me happy again.

The place I was working at the moment was a nightmare. While some of the colleagues were nice, others only wanted to see you fail. I stayed at the job only because of the manager. This kind person ended up helping me with a contract for Oliver.

I found a house to rent, and when Oliver came, we moved there.

Lydia, my little dolly, cried, not understanding why I was no longer going to be living with her. I went to visit her, and sometimes we kept her overnight. She did not like Oliver in the beginning, but he had a way with children and knew how to please them. In a short time, she took to him.

There were a lot of things I did not notice about Oliver. I just walked happily alongside him. I was so blind.

He did not like the simple job I found for him. It was not ideal, but he needed a job. I found it to help him out.

Moreover, because I had a second job, I was tired, but I needed to listen to all his complaints. Because he was unhappy, we were arguing. About every little thing.

"It would have been better if you had stayed living at your sister's and let me rent the house," he told me one day.

I replied, "When would we see each other? With two jobs taking all my time."

He said something about not liking to rely on me.

I was so in love, I did not understand that he wanted to be on his own, without me.

One moment he was laughing and joking, and the next one, he was accusing me of forcing him to leave the bank and work in a horrible place with stupid people. I knew what the situation was like there. I told him to stay there for three months because it would be unpleasant, for me, if he quit right way. The town was small, and the manager was a friend of Alessandro's. I did not want to create an unpleasant situation for my family, and it was unfair to my boss, who was so kind and made such an effort for Oliver. It was impossible those days to find someone who would help obtain a work visa. Despite me explaining all this, Oliver did not understand it. He had not seen all the hard work that was done for him; he only had to accept the contract and come.

Within two months, he developed carpal tunnel syndrome in his right hand. I was mute about it. I saw him suffering though.

Also, he was missing his daughter and family. He kept accusing me of taking him from them. I was to blame for everything, in his eyes.

In the first two months, he made friends, but it was hard to find a new job even with his network.

I felt hopeless.

My family could see our trouble. They told me to let him go because he did not love me enough. But I did not listen to them; I did not like them interfering.

At the time, I thought it was all my fault, and my fault only. I believed I attracted negativity to him, and to myself. I felt my love would be enough to heal him from his wounds. The truth was far more foreboding than I ever imagined.

I was lost, tired, and broken inside; I wanted a moment of peace. I knew this story must end.

Oliver was ready to go back home to Romania. I had the feeling he hated me. Though it was not my fault about all his trouble at home and work, he made me feel as if it was.

On top of all the issues at home, I brought a shadow of unease about foreigners into my work. My manager even told me he appreciated me a lot because I was a hard-working woman, but men from my country were strange. He went on to tell me my boyfriend did not deserve me. I was happy he did not pester me about Oliver quitting.

Now that I had bought a car, it was easier for me to travel to my jobs and to interviews as well. In a few months, I found another job, and I felt a bit better.

My new job was two-fold. I worked at a supermarket, during the day, from 7 a.m. to 2 p.m. Then in a pub, during the evening, from 5 p.m. until midnight or 2 a.m. I worked a lot, obviously. My schedule didn't allow for very much sleep.

For three hours—from 2 p.m. to 5 p.m.—I was free for lunch, and a friend living nearby invited me to her house. She was from my country; a beautiful woman with a big heart. We ate and spent time together for months, along with her little daughter, in their cosy cottage.

The supermarket/pub owner was kind, and I felt like part of the family. However, despite the fact that I loved the jobs, but my boss did not pay my annual leave. For how much he appreciated my hard work, he was not willing to *treat* me as his own family. I understood the situation, but I was not happy to be seen as a 'foreigner.' I talked to my boss, but he became upset and told me he could not afford to pay me more. Instead, he gave me help with some papers to buy a new car. This was better than nothing.

A friend offered me a week of work as a translator for a French specialist. I accepted; the pay was good, and I was on unpaid annual leave. I needed to work. I had no way to go to see my father again. I wanted to see Granny as well, but I could not afford to lose this chance.

I loved French, and I adored this job. I was the French translator for a nuclear specialist. He had a colleague from England, with his own translator, a guy born in the UK. We all spent time together in the office for four hours, and then at a restaurant for lunch. After lunch, the specialists had work to do, and the translators were free.

I met an English specialist, JC, on the first day—at our meal. We were introduced to each other by the French translator. When JC took my hand, we both got a kind of little electric shock, and we let go of each other's hand quickly, confused.

JC was a very tall man, with grey hair, incredible blue eyes—bright and intelligent. If I dared to look at him, I saw an image of him and I walking on a green path. I could not picture where it was, but the feeling made me shake all over. My heart stopped when I was in front of him. I felt stupid, and my stomach was in my mouth. I could not feel my legs, and I needed to have a sit. It was a kind of deja-vu; I did not understand what was happening.

Maybe I knew him from the other life? Was it possible? Why did I have a feeling we had some unexplained connection?

JC sat opposite me at the table. Though I did not understand English much, I did make out what he was talking about. A beautiful wife with Italian features—dark hair and eyes—and an only son, an intelligent and wonderful boy. His voice was music to my ears, and I tried to calm myself and breathe at a reasonable pace.

He was too old for me, why was I so involved? Why did I react to him as if I liked him? He was an older man; was I crazy? It was as if we have known each other before. But when? In the other life, maybe? I talked to myself as I was driving the car home.

I told my friend, Maria, about him and she laughed at me. I insisted my body was shaking in his presence, and that was how I felt in the presence of someone I liked. It was always hard to fall in love with someone, and now I was reacting as if I was in love.

All week, the same thing happened. I went to the office in the morning. We went to lunch together, where JC did not talk directly to me. Yet strange vibrations ran through me. Then after going home in the afternoon, I would think more about him. I thought I would never be so fortunate as to have a man like him near me.

Even the people around us said, "We can cut the air with a knife when you and JC are together."

I was relieved when the week finished, and I could go back to my routine, to my crazy life. I would not have to see him every day anymore as he was also going home—to England.

"Adios (goodbye), JC!" I wouldn't see him for 20 years.

I was back in the pub, and the work was pleasant with my bosses—two males. I loved them like my brothers. We were a good team. On weekends, singers performed live concerts, and the pub was full; I worked a lot.

Men sometimes invited me out with them. I became fed up and sad, too tired to argue with them. I saw some of them coming for a pizza with their families, and later they would return to try to get a date with me. I despised these people! I told them what I thought about what they were doing, though I was sure lots of them did not understand or care. Like they considered me a bloody foreigner who dared to refuse someone like them. I was always polite as this was now my only a job, my way to pay my bills. I knew I deserved more than how I was being treated by the patrons at this job.

Some of my friends came into the pub with new people. There was someone I liked—I felt something strange around him. His name was Luca. We became friends, and we talked for hours on end.

He and his wife were separated because of his behaviour. He deceived her by finding another woman, and now she hated him. Apparently, his wife had told him he was old and needed to think about their children, but she pushed him away from their intimate life. He missed his family, but she refused to talk to him.

I told him though I enjoyed our conversations, and his friendship, I would like to find someone relationship-free. I helped him with advice to impress the wife. I had lots of ideas, and he tried everything. Things started to work for him, but not for long.

One night, some friends asked me to go to bingo in a town nearby. We had a good time, laughing and talking for two hours. We were amazed by one of the girls who kept winning.

I met up with Luca and his friend, Matteo, who was 10 years older than I was. He looked very calm and composed; I felt comfortable near him.

I loved the feeling of 'calm.' Probably because it was the one thing missing in my life at the time. I was working impossible hours. There was no time for a boyfriend or even eating. My life was busy. It seemed I was always running. There was a constant pain in my stomach, and I knew I needed to slow down.

Matteo, nicknamed Matt, talked only to me, and I realized he was interested in me. After two hours more hours, my group was ready to go home. I noticed Matt watching me until I was out of his sight.

Being as tired as I was, I was ready for bed. Bingo was actually annoying to me; I went for the company. Plus, I met Matt. I knew I would see him soon again. He was reticent, and I sensed the kind of quiet that only a feline had, keeping calm when going after his prey. My senses were again sounding alarm bells, telling me 'stay away.' I wanted to get him out of my mind so I could sleep.

The next evening, Luca called me, asking if I would like to meet his friend again. I asked him if he thought it was a good idea—if Matt was okay.

"He is an excellent friend, but he never talks about his private life. I know he is separated, but no more details. If you think he is a womaniser, I tell you he is not. He is a lovely person, try to get to know him, and you can decide for yourself. I would be happy if you two were together," said Luca.

I decided I would give a try; I could not stay lonely forever.

I was busy, so I met Matt the following week. We had dinner together and took a walk near the sea. He made me laugh—a lot. We both knew we needed more time, but we liked each other. That much was clear.

He was an electrical engineer who specialised in solar panels; he loved his job.

The one thing I was not keen about was he was separated, not divorced. His wife lived in their house with their six-year-old son. Their adopted daughter, who was 12, spent most of her time with his wife's mother. His wife has a new boyfriend who would soon move in with her. *"Happily, she has a boyfriend,"* I thought.

Matt now lived in a flat, near the sea, on his own. As he was swamped with his work; it was tough to meet someone. *"Fair enough,"* I thought as I was in the same boat.

For three months, we dated, going for lunches, dinners, and ice cream near the sea. I wondered if Matt liked me enough because he never invited me somewhere private —his home or mine. He kissed me, but I thought it was strange he never wanted more.

I told my best friend this, and she laughed, "If he invited you to his home, you would have said, like all men he wants only a thing! If not, he must have a problem? You don't know what you want; this is your problem. Maybe he is a gentleman! Hahahaha!"

"Maybe he is not interested in sex. Could he be gay? I am fed up with all this 'gentleman' business. Maybe I am not enough for him. Perhaps he just likes talks and have a partner for meals, and that is it," I countered.

"I think you need a doctor. For your head, I mean. You have met a nice person, and you want him to be a pig!"

We then rambled about our dreams and hopes, having fun until late in the night.

I tried to see my niece, Lydia, whenever possible. She always accused me I worked too much. She was also upset because I was living so far away.

"It is hard to find a job near to you," I explained, but she was a child—she did not understand.

I hoped she understood that I loved her, and that was the absolute truth. I had never loved a child as I loved her. She was and would forever be a big part of my heart. We had a permanent connection that would last forever. It was like I was her 'other mother.' I cherished all the moments with my sister and my niece, but I was busy; therefore, we could only see each other once a month or less.

I was worried about her mental health because she had problems at school. Her colleagues called her 'cicciabomba' (that is 'fatso' in English). She was a sweet girl, brilliant, but because she was overweight, the other children called her names. She suffered emotionally, and she could not find peace. I empathized with her. I wanted to cut her colleague's tongues out. Children could be so cruel and did not always understand the harm inflicted on others. Lydia was the most beautiful girl in the entire world, and I would do whatever it took to make her believe it!

"My love, you are a little girl—not skinny, not fat—but one day you will look precisely how you want—a beautiful, thin lady all these wicked people will envy. I promise you," I told her as I covered her in a million kisses.

"I hope so, Aunty. I am fed up, and I want to kill myself," confessed my sweet little girl.

My sister cried when I told her. She admitted to me she was even having a hard time. She needed to talk to her daughter a lot and tried to cheer her up. Educating children was a hard job; I could see how difficult it is for my sister. A mother must always be careful and loving, friend and therapist, and so much more.

Matt was working impossible hours, yet he still found time to meet me, even when he was far from my city. When Matt was working near me, I could see him more often. One evening, after we had ice cream on the beach, he asked me if I wanted to see his flat near. Finally!

"Sure," I replied. I had wanted to for a while.

Once, inside, he told me I could have a shower. (In Italy, leaving near the sea, you were always full of sand; you needed to have showers more than usual.) I became nervous all of a sudden. Matt appeared careful, not very loving with me as if frightened to scare me somehow.

He got into the shower after.

When he was in the bathroom, his phone binged to notify him he received a message, and I could not help but look at it. The phone was in front of me, on the table. It was a woman. She was sorry he broke up with her, but she understood he was in love with someone else and appreciated his honesty. Good! I knew he would communicate in difficult situations—a point for him. Usually, people stayed stuck in a relationship because one felt sorry for the other person or someone was not enough brave to open the dialogue.

He read the message when he came back into the lounge. Without even a grimace, he placed the phone back on the table.

"Would you like to watch a film or are you tired?" he asked me.

"We can watch a film, but not something long, I have to get up early tomorrow," I answered.

We watched only half of the film. I went home in the morning, before going to work.

He was not gay after all, and I had one of my most fantastic nights in years.

❦

Matt found me a job at his friend's office. I had been a translator before, for his friend, Mark. I met his partner (or wife), Diana—a beautiful, tall, dark, very modern woman, with expensive taste—judging by her original Vuitton bag.

A young foreign woman and an Italian one worked in the office as well. I felt connected, from the beginning, with the Italian one, Nada, who had a transparent and robust personality. I did not like another one, Lea, who was kissing everyone's ass, especially Diana's. Lea was the kind of person who told everyone what they wanted to hear. She did not have a backbone, and she was awful. I once witnessed her begging like a little child for the boss to pardon her when she did something the boss had not approved. Day after day, I witnessed a jealous and mischievous Lea undermining Nada's credibility, and I could not believe it was working. I realized Lea hated that Diana kept Nada as a confident and friend, and Lea wanted this position. So young and such a bitch!

Diana often took us out—to eat somewhere nice or to buy us cosmetics or other things. I was impressed with how much money she spent on us. She had a good heart but did not have the nose for bad people.

It felt, somehow, like Diana was trying to buy our friendship. I did not want to be Diana's puppet, but there was not much I could do about it. She was the boss. You did what she wanted, or you were out. I loved the job, but I was wary of my bosses.

I noticed Diana always wanted to be near a tall, blond man when we had a break in the cafeteria. It was so apparent! I was not sure what game she was playing, but it felt like she had an affair with the man. I tried not to judge, but I was confused about what to think about her. She was interrogating me a lot about the time I was a translator for her husband and tried to find out if he met women or did other things. I supposed she and Mark had a peaceful marriage on the surface only. I did not tell her about him and his women. I knew his taste for whores (prostitutes); sometimes, he acted like a stupid Italian businessman, who thought money was the key to everything. He liked to 'buy' women, but I also knew he loved Diana and was very proud of her.

I told Matt about this situation one night. I thought it was a casual conversation, a regular talk, between a couple, however, within a few days, I found myself treated like a criminal at work.

Diana and Lea both interrogated me about how Mark found out about the affair with the blond man. Did I like Mark? Was I jealous? I could not believe what was happening; I told Diana I talked about what I noticed with Matt, in private, and that was it.

I had never felt so unhappy; I was so upset with Matt. He went directly to his friend to tell him what I said, without thinking about the consequences it would have for me. I knew it was my fault for gossiping, but I could not change things now.

In the office, the situation was out of my hands, but I took my responsibilities very seriously. Therefore, I could not leave at that moment. In one week, we had to be in Bucharest for a trade show, where we would have a stand. Diana booked the hotel, bought the flight tickets, and I had decided to finish my job properly, before leaving that bloody office.

The trade show was going well, but Mark was behaving like a jerk—everywhere we went. The taxi drivers complained about his callousness, and they did not understand how I could work for such an asshole. I was ashamed, but I kept quiet. If not, I feared I would explode by telling my senseless boss what I thought about him. I only wanted to do my job and go back home to Italy.

After three days, Mark told me he did not understand where I went every night after work. I felt I had enough. My job was during the time of the trade show, not at night when he was meeting women.

Every night I was meeting Ciel, who was now an actress in a very well-known theatre in Bucharest. I watched her play, and we went to eat somewhere after.

I was so disgusted with Mark when he questioned me about my free time; I told him all my feelings. He was in shock; he could not believe I dared to do this. I even told him I was quitting when we went back to Italy.

Only Nada understood me in the office, but I knew even her days there were ending. I was done, and she would leave shortly after me. Lea had concocted a plan to get Nada in trouble.

Back in Italy, proud I did an excellent job at the trade show, I quit this office nightmare.

I planned to work in a hotel, and I would be happy to do simple tasks but to retain my peace of mind.

The boss was a splendid woman who gave me more important duties shortly after I started. Even at this new job, life was difficult because of jealous colleagues. They did not understand why I was so appreciated—being promoted so quickly.

What they did not realise was, in the morning I was a purchasing manager. For the rest of the day, I cleaned inside the hotel and outside, performed as a barista, waitress, or whatever else was needed. This was why I had a better salary. I was only sleeping two or three hours per night, and I kept going this way for years.

When working around the hotel, tourists, mostly French, looked for me because I was the only person who spoke French in the hotel.

"Why are you cleaning when you talk so well in other languages? At the reception desk, it is impossible to have a chat in French. Instead, the cleaner knows the language. Your bosses must be so blind," customers were pointing out.

However, I didn't like working reception, or maybe not this particular reception. I would have been nose to nose with the boss all day, and I wasn't always the most obedient employee in the world.

My boss's brother took charge of the hotel. He cut our hours and started to pay the salary after two months. My colleagues were all frightened, but they would not take action. I needed to fight every month for my wage, and I was livid when my new boss suggested I was a nice woman, and I should find a man to take care of me financially. I quickly told him I did not need a man; I needed my wages on time.

Matt decided we should move in together in a small flat in a city where he would work for three years. I was more than happy to change my life. I needed some rest because the last year was hard. I moved with Matt to a small city near the sea. I was happy to be with him. I could have my morning walks in such a fantastic place. I was not too far from my family and Lydia, and on the weekends, I could see them. I felt my life was taking a new and relaxing path.

Dad was always in my mind; we chatted on the phone. He now had a new partner and seemed happy. I had only gone home three times in the last 15 years, and he did not like that. However, because I still kept a kind of hate towards him, when I was at home, we argued a lot. Plus, I did not want to see another woman in our house. I felt it was an insult to my mother's memory. I understood Dad had health problems and needed help, but it was still painful to think of someone else in the place where Mom worked a lot. I also knew how much Mom wanted to see the house finished, and the care she took in placing every piece of furniture where it was.

My father's partner seemed nice when I eventually met her, but she would never be like my mother, who kept all very clean and tidy. She was a far cry from what Mom was. I wanted to keep everything the same; my lovely mother was dead, and she would never come back. My heart was still full of love for her, and I wanted to stay away from my father's new arrangement. I was so unhappy. I still blamed my Dad for Mom dying early. I reasoned Mom would still be here if Dad had behaved better.

But then, I asked myself, who am I to judge him? He knew what was best for himself, and life was sad when you got older and lonelier. He had his own sins, but he was also an intelligent and creative person; he liked to share this all with someone else. Judgement was not up to me. It was unfair of me to expect him to live the last part of his life as a monk. He had health problems—acid reflux. And I doubt my mother, his wife, wanted him to suffer by himself. Mom loved him—unconditionally—and I knew she would have wanted him healthy and happy, even if someone else had to take care of him.

I knew all this, deep down in my heart. Yet, I was still conflicted. I wanted Dad happy, but I did not want him to have a new partner. It was a love/hate relationship. Which would prevail?

> "…sometimes good things fall apart so better things
> can fall together."
> Marilyn Monroe

CHAPTER 6

Wind of Change

I had been living with Matt now for two years, as a couple. Life was peaceful and quiet. He did not drink and never shouted. Instead, he was always lovely and appreciative. It felt like heaven.

Though I did not have a permanent job; Matt had lots of solicitor friends, and they often needed documents translated from French or Romanian to Italian. The money was good, and my partner urged me to do what I liked.

I enrolled in university studying French and English. I enjoyed every moment, and I was thrilled with my new career choice. I made new friends, and every day I learned something new. I spent time with Julia and Roxana, the first was from Kyrgyzstan and the second from Ukraine. Julia was the pragmatic one, and Roxana was one with her legs on the ground.

Both women had a Christian background, and they were religious. It was still hard for me to talk about God. I was upset with God. My father never stopped drinking—well he did but only for short periods—and my mother died so young. In my upbringing, I was taught God was kind, helpful, and protective.

My life experience taught me otherwise; He was ruthless. Julia's beliefs varied, she seemed to choose only 'rules' that suited her needs and choices. Roxana was sincere, transparent, and her heart reflected God in all she did.

My personal beliefs regarding God were unclear—I believed, but I was angry. Yet, I found myself praying sometimes, like before a hard exam. When I realised what I was doing, I told myself, *"You are so hypocritical. You laugh with superiority when people pray. Yet you pray when you feel danger or trouble."*

I think maybe we have a mechanism inside that triggers praying automatically when we feel some kind of danger. The awful thing was, after a 'problem' disappeared, I forgot about God and my prayers. I felt selfish and duplicitous. Maybe this two-faced personality has to do with astrology because I am a Gemini—the twins. Maybe my one face does not believe in God, and the other is religious instinctively. I was like a savage who only acted by instinct.

I knew inside I had a fight preparing about this topic. Yet I avoided thinking about it when I was tired, in the way Scarlet O'Hara used to: "Tomorrow, I'll think of some way…after all, tomorrow is another day."

My language university was a lot of work, but I enjoyed every moment. It was completely different from my other career choice. When I was doing economics, it was something I *had* to do—because everyone told me it was right for me. Now, it was a great pleasure, because I *wanted* to do it, I didn't *have* to do it. This experience opened my eyes to the joy of doing something I loved.

Matt was happy for me, especially because he took lots of work around the country and was away most of the time. Sometimes I went with him, but I had an extra job teaching a little boy nearby different languages; I could not afford to be away for long. Moreover, I was taking English lessons with Julia and Roxana. A colleague who lived in the UK for years was teaching us. English caused me trouble; I never studied it at school. I did not even know any basics, so I had to work extra hard to learn it.

After a long chat with my Romanian auntie, I found out I could get a job in England. I even had a contact there, a woman my auntie knew. I decided to go try it out for three months; at the time, I did not have a permanent job. Matt was not happy about it, but he let me do what I wanted. He knew I loved him, and he knew I loved Italy. He hoped I would come back quickly from 'The North Pole,' as he called the UK.

I was sure my skills in English would get better there as I would be immersed in the language, and what better way to learn? In three months, I would return to my walks near the sea, sunny days, and fantastic food.

I forgot I was a slant driller by instinct. Fate had hidden something from my sight. Everything would change with this decision, but I was not yet aware of this.

My contract was for three months in Gloucestershire. The company I would be working for paid for my flight, which was good because I knew I could have found a cheaper one.

Things appeared too good to be true; something nagged at me from the back of my mind. I called Danna, my auntie's friend, and asked about the salary.

Even though she seemed happy with her job, I quickly realized she was underpaid. I knew, but she was oblivious.

I also was worried about the staff house. After having my own flat, I needed my privacy; I wanted a room to myself. It was not that simple, I was told. I needed to wait for it, and it depended on where I would be transferred to work.

After living in Italy, I saw things differently. Danna went to the UK from Romania, and she perceived things from another point of view. Not just about her employment, but everything, it seemed.

Trying not to be bothered too much about the wages and living situation, I continued forward. I felt I had to take advantage of this chance to improve my English.

One month before leaving for England, Matt was still working in the north. I was lonely at home. This seemed the perfect time to go see Dad. Lara, my sister, would be arriving too, with her family, three days after me. It would be helpful, emotionally, to be together again at 'home,' to spend time with Dad and visit friends and family.

The house seemed okay, but the yard was a mess. I had to call some people from the village to help clean it all. It was hard work, but once it was finished, I felt I had done something beautiful for Dad.

Lara wasn't there anymore so she couldn't take care of everything, but I knew she would understand what I had done.

Dad had done the design for the front garden, and it was perfect now. I even renewed the sidewalk. My father's partner, Eva, was happy with all the completed work. With money I lent her, she bought new tiles for the little cottage kitchen. She would need to do the manual work putting in the tiles, but she had all the tools to do it.

Tired, I went outside and sat on the stairs. From the back-door stairs, I could enjoy the view. The front yard looked tidy and appeared inviting now. Surely Eva and Dad would now want to spend time outside.

My father and Eva were having an afternoon rest in the cottage, when I heard Dad talking with 'the voice' I did not like. It was the voice that made me want to leave and stay away. He had been drinking.

"What was she thinking, my daughter? She threw some money in the yard, and now I need to kiss her hands? Who does she think she is?" His voice carried out to me.

"George, please! It is all so beautiful. Don't make her feel bad. She wants you to live in a nice place. She could do something else with her money. Be nice to her, please," Eva pleaded with him.

"I don't care. They think having money makes them gods. Ha! I am fed up," he continued.

I still sat on the stairs outside. My body was becoming heavier and heavier. I could not move, my stomach was hurting, and I had, what felt like, a big stone sitting on my chest. My throat was dry, probably from all the silent screaming inside my heart. I wanted to be far away from this house at that moment. Even the thought of my sister joining us could not warm the coldness my father expelled with his words. I was upset and heartbroken.

Later, Eva tried to cheer me up. I do not remember what I said to her; I still cannot remember a single word. All I knew was I wanted to get away from him.

The next morning, Alessandro and Lara showed up. My sister was not happy when I told her I was going back to Italy so soon. Alessandro gave her a lift, but he needed to be at work the next morning. They appreciated all the jobs I had done in our parents' home. Lara wanted me to stay with her for a couple of days, but I could not be there anymore. She understood, but she was sad nonetheless. I decided to go back to Italy with Alessandro.

When I had returned to Italy, I needed a holiday from my holiday. I missed Chloe and got the idea to go see her and her daughter in Geneva. The thought raised my spirits and made me happy. I loved Geneva; sightseeing was something I really enjoyed.

Though I felt a bit better, my thoughts returned to my father. I could not understand why Dad behaved this way with me. I wanted to make him happy, yet all my work seemed to make him angry instead. It did not matter how hard I tried; he was never pleased. Thinking and rethinking, I knew he did not mean what he said. He was drunk.

He was always independent—the one to do things around the house. Now he was older and did not have the economic power he used to have. He resented his daughters doing things for him. Even if they just wanted what was best for him. I wanted to ensure he had what he needed, so he could live a good life. Again, I hated him and loved him at the same time.

My week with Chloe and her daughter ended too soon, and I was back in Italy. Matt smiled, but he was not happy with my next trip—to the UK. He asked if I was pleased with my summer. I was grateful he understood my need to go to the UK and did not try to stop me or change my decision. I thought Matt would have preferred if I settled down, but he gave me my space. He never imposed, but he asked me what would keep me near him permanently. My answer was, simply, "Your divorce." We talked a lot about this, and I knew the reasons he held back, but it was still something that kept me unhappy.

We could not continue; we broke up.

In July, I flew to England.

༄

I spent a week in Gloucestershire for the training, driving lessons (for the other side of the road), and job shadowing.

The city was strange; all the houses looked the same. You could get lost easily when wandering around. Driving was scary to me; some lanes were narrow, but I managed alright.

At the training, there were 15 people from different countries. There was a couple, Janet and Radu, from my region in Romania and I thought they were cute together. I quickly learned people from the office avoided them, if they could, because the couple was very demanding. Apparently, Janet complained about *everything*, and the bosses were fed up. She was undoubtedly the boss in this relationship; Radu just followed her like a dog, trusting what she decided. I liked her determination to get what she wanted, but I became tired when listening to them for too long. But they were young and beautiful, and they were amusing sometimes.

The teacher talked at a reasonable pace, and most of the time, I understood her. Sometimes I heard just a kind of mumbling, and I felt lost. I started shadowing, which means following a colleague when working—to learn what to do, like going to people's houses. You were assigned different locations during the day, and you spent between 15 minutes and one hour with an older person who needed help in their home. You needed to make them a hot drink, cook a meal, give medication, help with personal care, or simply talk to them, in some cases.

The people we were helping varied in their moods; some were lovely and others grumpy. My English was rubbish, but they helped me. I loved that every house had a library, and people often had a book in hand.

After watching others work, it was soon my turn to work on my own. I had a driver assigned who drove me to all the places I needed to go. I started my first day; it quickly became a very curious day.

The first call in the morning was a lady who needed help to wash and dress. She had an operation on her knee. I was given half an hour for this. Once I was in the house, I found the lady in bed, happy to see me. The room had an astonishing library, on three of the walls, but my eye caught notice of lots of dust on the shelves, and the books seemed to cry their freedom from that heaviness. I did not have time to dust, and it was not one of my tasks. I needed to help the lady with a wash, so I asked where the bathroom was, so I could get hot water. When I opened the bathroom door, I felt as if I was entering Dickens's world, precisely, *The Great Expectations*. There was a thick spiderweb from the sink to the window and shower. I had never seen anything like it in my life. And maybe even if I had been told about it, I would have never believed the story.

I looked for a broom to clean up the mess. I found it was hard work. It took lots of time to make space near the sink and to get the liquid soap, near the window.

Once I was all done, I had a confrontation with my driver, who lectured me about timing, duties, and rapidity. I spent more than forty-five minutes in the house, and that was bad, according to my driver. Even after I explained the situation, he did not care. I needed to respect the time written on my rota (roster/schedule), which was, in this case, only half an hour.

I started to wonder what kind of help this was if we let these older people remain living in poor conditions. Each house I went to, I noticed houses needed a deep cleaning, and I wanted to change something. It was impossible, I knew. I needed to arrive on time for the next call, and most of the time, you could not because of the traffic or time spent to find an address. But was the care I was providing help?

I was to be transferred to a new staff house in Oxfordshire along with the curious couple I met on training. Janet called me when she arrived at the new home to tell me it was an excellent, clean house. I was pleased to hear this. She told me two other ladies were living there—one from our country, Anda, and one from Greece, Helen.

"Oh, God, please help me," I thought. I did not like to share a house, and now I would need to share a room. I had a terrible feeling there would be problems. My gut reaction was usually right; I was certain that problems would arise.

After a few days, it was my turn to go. I handed in my car keys, took the car assigned to me, and put the new address on my satnav (satellite navigation). I felt lost from the start. After half an hour, I found myself in the countryside, in a narrow lane, halted by a big harvester—there was no place to go on either side of it. Being as exhausted as I was, I started to cry and put my head against the steering wheel. I felt stupid and useless.

The harvester driver solved my problem, making space for me to follow the road. When he pulled over, he motioned for me to stop as well. He then set up my satnav properly and encouraged me to continue to drive. I was soon back on the motorway, happy and more confident.

The house looked nice—part of a new complex. This made me smile. I was sharing a room with Helen. Although she seemed like a nice person, I still was not happy to have a roommate. My smile disappeared.

Helen was gorgeous and tried to put me at ease. One positive was she was not a young girl (who could be loud and temperamental).

Anda and I became friends right away. It seemed our three other housemates were jealous. It was like we had been friends for years, though I did not understand how the law of attraction worked with friendships.

109

She worked late one night, so when I cooked, I made sure to make a plate for her too. Janet laughed and told me to let Anda cook for herself. Janet and her boyfriend did not like Anda very much. They were both selfish, doing things that suited only themselves. I did not understand them; I was happy only when sharing—when I could make others happy. To them, this was stupid, but I could not change my nature. I knew they would be moved far away in a short time because they were concentrated only on themselves.

The salary was insufficient; I was in misery. Coming from Italy, where I had a very nice life and made more money, I was used to eating healthy and well. However, because the salary was so low at this job, I could not maintain the standard of living I was used to. I was lost with money, and I was not good with budgeting. Anda laughed because she was very organised and knew how to stick to a budget. She could make her paycheck cover everything she needed. I, on the other hand, questioned why I was living here, in England, where I couldn't even eat properly. At that moment, I wanted to go back to Italy, but I did not want to appear as a weak person—one who bailed when things were tough.

The couple was very competitive and keen on making money. Anda, Helen, and I got in 'trouble' if any of us worked more hours than them per week. This upset me sometimes, but I admired Janet's desire to make her 'family' happy. She wanted money to marry this handsome boy, even though everyone could see he would be trouble for her, resulting in her being unhappy.

She was a beautiful young lady who wanted a handsome husband. More to show up at fancy places with, I feared, than because she loved him. She was a forceful woman—like a hurricane— but she used her force in the wrong way, one that would ultimately destroy her.

Her and I sometimes talked about her relationship with Radu, or rather, she spoke, and I listened.

I knew some couples smacked each other, some even severely. Often partners in these types of relationships would not accept outside advice. In all my past relationships, I made the mistake of not listening to others. Not that any of my partners was physically abusive. Only when Janet showed me the bruises around her neck, did I tell her to have the courage to let him go. She would find another soulmate.

The next day, when I was on the double with Anda at work, Radu called me. He gave me an entire lecture about relationships and love and told me to keep my advice to myself.

These two people were dangerous, I realised. I did not look for gossip, but obviously, they talked, or rather argued. That same evening, when we were all back from work, this couple seemed to be more in love than ever. Maybe she lied to me; maybe they had hard sex—perhaps they were sadists. What I wanted was to make them disappear from my life. I did not need the drama.

The time came for me to book an appointment with my insurance agent. The office was in Oxford. Though I was frightened to drive in this busy city, I was also very excited to go because I thought I could get some sightseeing in. I was lucky to have an entire day off. Though worried about my English, I was sure I would be fine, able to answer all the questions.

I had to wait for one month for my trip to Oxford, and in the meantime, I did my job. The English countryside was amazing, with its small villages—little gems of history and architecture.

The manager changed my usual rota a bit, and now I was working in new places around Oxford. My housemates were curious about the changes as I excitedly told them how friendly people were, and how beautiful the scenery was. I suppose they did not believe me, but I did not care too much. They heard my rota was changed; maybe it was not enough hours for them. I was satisfied, and that was the most important thing.

Some of my ladies waited for me with cakes, and everyone loved me.

One day, going to visit two ladies in a small village near Witney, I found myself on a road where two thatched cottages were having their roofs fixed. I had an hour break, so I went to take some photos. Because of the location, I needed to take pictures from the other side of the road. Being in front of a cottage gave me a strange feeling. I could not move; I thought maybe in another life I lived here. Though I was enraptured by the view, I needed to go to work. Otherwise, someone might see me and wonder what I was doing there, watching the house. As I walked away, I felt sorrow, like when I was living at my house in Romania, and I left for university—with Mom waving to me.

In the evening, I told Anda about my day, the cottage, and the feelings I had. She thought I was too excited about England. She listened to me, then it was her turn to be passionate about the places she had seen that day. She also loved everything about England. Every day, we exchanged our curiosities and happiness about places or things we had seen. Chatting to Anda was always relaxing. I could forget about the problems with the couple. When they were there, they toxicated the atmosphere talking about money, properties they owned, expensive cars they left home...boooooooring, for me.

Helen was in love. I knew the man she was in love with because of our job. Everyone from the staff house had visited him in his home, helping him as carers. He was an intelligent man, but his house was a mess, and he never let us doing anything about it. Helen was spending more hours with him, and I noticed he was happier. He always asked about her or talked about her. The company policies did not allow us to be too friendly with the residents. However, it was impossible to work like a robot— without emotions. I understood because they were almost the same age, and she was without a husband.

When I was working with Michael, the resident Helen loved, I asked him about her. He appeared thrilled about her, but a bit frightened because his nurse was against this kind of relationship. I was confused; I asked what the nurse had to do with him liking someone. This was a personal matter, and only he could choose. I understood all the rules at our job, but they cannot define who we loved. Michael was also worried about his son's reaction, though Michael appeared independent with decisions about his life. I did not understand. He explained that his son might be unhappy with him having a partner because he owned property. Property his son would inherit, assuming he did not remarry.

Maybe it was the first time in my life when I realised that once I was older, I would be the only one making decisions about my life as I did not have children.

It was also the first time I had seen myself as a selfish person, thinking about my father and his need to have a partner. Why do some children see their parents as their properties? As people who need to ask permission to do whatever they decide about their own life?

It was true that sometimes, getting older meant people could have health issues, or may make an ill-advised decision too quickly. Older folks might make the wrong decisions, but we needed to let them travel the path to their happiness. Most of the time, we base our choices or guidance, so the outcome is to our advantage; we may be sure our old parents lived their lives, and that should be enough for them.

In this case, we may believe they are too old to want to love. How sad is that?

I listened to Helen for weeks, talking about her love, happy for her. In the house, the couple started to have to say about this story, mostly bad things. They thought it was all wrong, and told her to give up because he was not suitable for her. Helen kept going with her decision to be with her love one day. I hoped it will have a happy ending. She was very suggestible. I advised her to do what she felt was right, yet the couple was saying different things to her.

My trip to Oxford day finally arrived. I drove to Oxford Centre, found a place to park the car, and I arrived in time for my appointment. All was going well. I saw a coffee shop and decided I was ready for an Italian expresso—one that would change my life. I will remember that day forever!

CHAPTER 7

The One and Only...

All I was thinking about was a creamy, short, perfumed expresso; I was dying to have an Italian coffee. I walked toward the coffee shop, stretching out my hand to open the door. Before I could, the door opened and in front of me was a tall man who just stood there, not moving. I did not look at his face; I was preoccupied with thoughts of a delicious coffee. I simply wanted to enter the shop. I did not understand what was he doing standing there, like a gunnysack. He let me go inside after a moment, but he stayed inside with his hand on the door. When I looked at his face, I felt my cheeks getting warm and reddish. That's when realized, *"Oh, gosh! I know him!"*

It would have been impossible to forget the two bright blue eyes staring from the most intelligent face I had ever seen. After 20 years, I still blushed looking into JC's eyes. He was older now but was *him*. He had a very imposing presence; tall and handsome; big blue eyes; and long, white hair. I knew he was the English specialist I worked with in Italy 20 years earlier. I felt my body warming up.

"I know you! You are from Italy. I do not remember your name, only that is an ancient name in your country of origin," he said to me, while looking directly in my eyes.

"JC? Am I right?" I grunted.

"You must be looking for an Italian coffee. Would you like me to keep you company?" JC inquired.

"Of course, so strange to meet you here," I replied.

"It was meant to be. I hardly ever come here, but today I had the feeling something good would happen."

He had never talked to me directly before. I was amazed by how happy I was suddenly. Given that we never had a conversation in Italy, I was delighted to have a chat with him.

November 14, I will remember on this day forever. We could not finish talking. There was a significant gap in time to cover. His beautiful wife had died six years prior, and his only son lived abroad, on another continent. I understood how lonely he was, but at the same time, I had the feeling he was happy with what life gave him. He did not complain about anything; he just told me things about himself. We had lots more coffee, even food, only to have a motive to be there together. Hours were flying by. It was almost dark outside, and I needed to go home. He did not drive but planned to take a taxi to his village near Oxford. I asked him if he wanted a ride back, and he was more than happy to accept.

Once in front of his house, I was in for another surprise. His house was the cottage I told Anda about. Too many coincidences were happening.

"Do you live here? Really?" I asked.

"This is my place, yes. Come see it," he replied, leading me toward it.

It was a small stone cottage, at least it looked small from outside. Once inside, the house was big enough, with a second garden in the back. It was very English in style, a bit untidy, wild, but still beautiful. I promised him I would come to visit again. He gave me his phone number and wanted my rota to be sure when I had a gap in my busy days. His face displayed a giant smile, as did mine. I felt peace and happiness near him, in addition to all the coincidences around us. From his lounge window, he waved to me as I was leaving. I could not wait to tell Anda everything.

Life is extraordinary, and you never know what surprise is around the corner.

Going home, I thought and rethought about all the coincidences. Whether coincidence or not, I was in front of him at the right moment. Or maybe, he was in front of me at the right moment. Five seconds later for either of us and poof. All gone! But I saw him again, after all these years, in the middle of England. Even more, he was living in the house I was so thrilled about. This was too much! The hours spent with him were so lovely and peaceful.

Anda soon heard all about the day. She was sure I would move from the staff house shortly. "I have never seen you so happy. You will go to stay with him, I know it."

"I am so exhausted. Today was too much for me. I like him, but we have quite an age gap between us. But I like him. Of course, I like him. I am crazy. I will go to revisit him. I know I enjoy every minute with him." I was like a young woman discovering her first love.

The couple and Helen sensed something going on with me, but I babbled some lie to them. I wanted to keep this happy moment for myself. It was not easy because Janet was very curious by nature, and she usually found a way to discover things.

As I was not yet sure of my situation with the job, I do not want to give anyone a reason to suspect I wasn't going to stay. I was not happy at work. In particular, I was not satisfied with the living situation in the staff house. And I missed Italy, Matt, my family, Lydia, the sea—everything. Only Anda knew my true feelings; I did not tell any of my other housemates that I hated the job and wanted to go home. I did not want to appear weak. But everyone could see my happy face today. Now they will guess what happened because I have a smile stamped on my face.

On my day off, I visited JC. The house seemed clean. It was dirty, but in a way that appeared okay. Yet, if you looked properly, it was a mess. The only neat thing there was the lounge, where a woman had dusted properly. JC helped me to put the kitchen in order and to clean the fridge. It took hours, but we were laughing and laughing, so we did not notice the time. He was the smartest person I had ever met. His sense of humour was subtle. I needed to get used to it. I did not always know when he was joking, or when it was for real. In his teasing manner, I recognized he was so happy I was there; he was mocking me with love.

He asked me about moving to his house. I would have my own bedroom. In exchange, I would clean and cook for him and, of course, spend time with him.

"I wouldn't mock the Sword of Destiny, JC. You want me to come to live in your house, but you don't like me cleaning and putting everything in order. I will unravel your universe here," I threatened.

He said he would help with my English and help me find a better job. I wanted to do it, and I knew I would soon enough. I did not worry about anything because I felt deep down that everything would be okay. I did not need time to think because, for the first time in my life, I felt at home and safe. I did not need time to settle any affairs. I did not need a friend's second opinion. I did not need to consider postponing the choice. Because I was sure that it was right.

Spending time with JC was wonderful. He asked me questions and vice versa. We would sit in the lounge, near each other. We rested in his comfortable armchairs after putting the house in order. He came near me and showed me how to use the armchair mechanism to get a better position.

Then he started with his third-degree questioning, "What would you like to do?"

"What do you mean? In my life? In my job?" I answered.

"Job."

"I don't know. For the moment, I do not speak enough English to be able to choose. I do not have enough money to do a course. I am not a specialist in anything. I am not good enough to learn new things. I am tired, ugly, and depressed at this moment and…"

"Stop! Sorry, you are so negative," he interrupted.

I tried to explain, "No, it isn't that. I am in a new country. I don't know how things will turn out. I don't have a personal car. My family and friends are far away…"

"You are all about the negative. If you want to do something, think positive, and start to do it."

"It's so simple to you…you don't understand…"

He did not let me finish my sentences and seemed stumped by my worries. "I have never seen someone so negative. You know only 'I can't, I am not good enough, I do not have this or that…'"

"It is easy for you to say. I am the one in a situation where I cannot move. If I quit this job, I won't have a car. And without a car, how would I get to work?"

I continued, "With my English, I do not understand what people are talking about most of the time. I watch TV with subtitles. Maybe I am too old to learn."

"Hahaha! I see I have to do some work with you on your self-esteem. You are a young, beautiful, and intelligent woman. You need to believe in yourself more. There is nothing wrong with you. Leave your job, come to live here, and I will give you a hand," JC stated.

He continued, "We are having a conversation right now, and I understand you. Your English is good, you need a little improvement. That takes time, but you are on the right path. Stop worrying."

Then he asked me straight out, "What would you like to do? When do you want to come live here, then?"

I was watching him, and I could not believe it. Everything was easy for him. He still did not understand. He had never been in my position: an immigrant with no money who spoke poor

English. My family was not nearby for support. And he had no knowledge about this new adventure I was on. I didn't answer him.

"Don't look at me like that. You didn't answer my question. What would you like to do?" he persisted.

"Write books," I finally responded. The words came out of my mouth without thinking. This was my secret dream; I lost my way for a while, but I had not forgotten.

"You will write a book and in English. I promise you," JC stated with conviction. From his armchair, he seemed like a king making decisions about people's lives.

I smiled, grateful for this wonderful man who cheered me up. I still thought writing a book would be impossible, but I felt happier. Thanks to JC. Despite all the stress with my job and the staff house, he managed to plant the seed of hope in my mind. Maybe I would be able to change my situation here. Even though my dream of writing a book in English seemed too much for the moment—even impossible—I could improve some things in my life. Perhaps I would become more confident. With JC as my English teacher, I was sure I could learn to speak better and to a higher standard.

I could even fall in love with this cold weather in England. In Romania, it was cold in winter, but the rest of the warm was nice and warm. Italy had the same warm temperature year-round. In England, all year, it was cold; the sun was always covered in clouds.

After a day with JC, even my job started to seem lovely.

I was quite curious about life in England. I wanted to know more about JC, his life, his likes and dislikes, and his opinion about everything. He was smart, calm, and so cute! I loved the way his face moved when he talked, and how he twiddled his fingers as if he was knitting when he was waiting for an answer—one he probably would not like.

"Do you believe in God?" he asked me one day.

"Why?" I inquired.

"Not why. Do you believe or not?"

"I don't know, really. I think not, but when I am in trouble, I want to believe. Hmmm. I do not believe in God. Do you have a scientific piece of evidence that God exists?"

JC laughed. "Good, you are not just a pretty face. I do not like to be near someone who bothers me to go to church and things like that."

"No problem, but I'd like to talk more about this. What are your ideas, your thoughts?" I turned the question back to him.

"We will talk then. What do you think about having supper with me now—next door?"

"What do you mean 'next door?'" *"Did one of his neighbours cook?"* I wondered.

"The pub. Next door. Would you go with me?" he explained.

"Thank you for the invite, but I must run home. Not that I am unhappy with this, but I need to sort out some papers, and I am starting work early in the morning." I tried to excuse myself.

"Will you come to live here?" he asked again, holding my hands in his.

"I will, soon." I kissed his face gently. Then I left.

Just thinking about JC, and I got in a better mood. It seemed we knew each other a lifetime ago. I could figure out what JC wanted simply from his movements or his facial expressions.

We did not need to talk all the time to enjoy being together. It was enough to be in the same room, watching TV. I was happy. He liked to tease and play as a child sometimes. When I went to visit one time, I brought him white chocolates—Rafaello. He offered me one in the beginning, but after that, he kept the box near him. If he saw my eye on the sweets, he would move the box slowly to his knee, keeping an eye on me the entire time. A childish, sly grin on his face. Like he was a child hiding his favourite toy from a colleague who wanted to play with it. All with a very furtive movement, watching me. I have never guessed inside this serious, old man was a little boy.

In the staff house, the situation was getting worse. Word of Helen's romance arrived at the manager.

The couple tried to persuade Helen to let go of everything. Now they were putting in her head that Michael was not suitable for her. They told her the situation was dangerous if she worked with him; she could be in big trouble. Helen was confused. She confessed, to me, about how wonderful it all was and that Michael told her he loved her, too, and they wanted to live together. They had a plan. She would clean and disinfect the house, take him out (he was always in bed or the wheelchair), and he would be the man he once was, again. They were both so happy about this perspective.

I sensed her joy and wished her all the best, but the next day, I was in trouble again, with the malevolent couple involved in this situation. The day I visited JC, they questioned me where I was and why I looked so happy. Without thinking twice, I told them Michael, Helen's man, gave me English lessons. However, I didn't have a chance to talk to Helen to explain the situation, and the couple went and told Helen I was trying to take Michael from her.

Helen believed them and was now upset with me. Despite my reassurances, she did not believe me. She wanted me to call Michael in front of her, without letting Michael know she was there. She wanted to hear what we talked about. I phoned Michael and had a chat with him. Michael talked about Helen—how much he was in love with her and how a beautiful person she was. My Greek friend jumped for joy; her mind was settled that I was not trying to steal her love from her.

The couple must have been black with hate at that moment, I knew they would not stop there. And I was right, they started in again the next day. They seemed to want everyone miserable.

Anda helped me move house. All the others in the staff house thought I was going for a job to live with a lady. Janet offered to take me there, but I managed to refuse. I wanted peace, and my version of peace included her far away from me. I did not hate her or anything, in fact, sometimes I liked her. It was tough to put up with her for an entire day though—when you had the feeling she was smiling, keeping a knife behind her back, ready to attack you at any minute.

It was November and cold outside. In JC's house, it was warm, and I had started a major cleaning. I had given up the job as a community carer. Now, I was his companion full time.

I cooked for JC, who was thrilled. He was in love with everything I put in front of him. I only cooked Italian, but not pasta he did not like. Sometimes he wanted lasagne but not often.

In my new living arrangement, I was happy. We even loved the same programs on TV. Talking to JC was a privilege.

I started English lessons on my own, on the internet. Every day I worked hard at learning, and I was improving in all my chats with JC. If I asked him clarification about a new word, he explained the meaning better than the Oxford Dictionary. He made terms clear and neat. And he was patient and willing to help. Even if I disturbed him when watching something he did not want to miss, he turned off the sound, listened carefully to me, and answered calmly. I adored him.

Anda came to see me when she could. I found out our manager told Helen to finish seeing Michael, and she was not allowed to work with him anymore. This made me very sad. And now, apparently, Helen was upset with me. I did not understand. Who knew what the 'wonderful two' told her? Helen was very suggestible. The couple could easily manipulate her. Regardless, I could not do anything about it.

Before Christmas, I went to the staff house with presents. Only Janet was there. Her boyfriend did not want to see me, and neither did Helen. I asked Janet about this. She said Helen was upset because of what I had done. Though Janet did not even hint at what I supposedly did to Helen. And Janet's boyfriend was upset because he thought I told the manager about him hitting her. Which I did not do.

Anda advised me not to bother with all the drama because they were all crazy in that house. I thought she knew more about the situation, but I did not press her for more information.

Life was good to me at the moment, why would I bother with strange people? Knowing I would be back near JC in an hour put a smile on my face, and my heart was pumping as if I was in a race. I decided, at that moment, to close the door on these people and go forward with my life.

Back at JC's, I decided to decorate. In the loft, I found everything I needed for Christmas. There was a Christmas tree, baubles, festoons, and even crackers. Our winter holidays were fantastic! He liked a Christmassy home. It was impressive to see him enjoying everything.

"I must have done something right in my life to deserve you. I never thought I would be so happy again," he told me, his blue eyes twinkling.

I felt the same way.

JC had an idea of how I could work on my English skills. He thought it would be useful to start an NVQ in health care to obtain a better salary. (In England, an NVQ is a National Vocational Qualification—a work-based way of learning. I now have an NVQ3 qualification, which is what I need to be a senior carer in health care, and I am paid better.) He found some providers, and I only needed to find a job to complete this. But this was something to do a bit later. I started after New Year's.

The course provider sent a book; I just need to work through it. I was beginning to learn. The first 20 pages were full of my red highlighter for translation of words I did not understand. After one month, however, my highlights became less frequent as my English had improved a lot. I felt more prepared and confident about the things a carer needed to do.

JC's son, CJ, came to visit him. He was a nice man—my age. He did not have issues with me living in his father's house, but we told him only that I was JC's carer. I did not tell him that JC and I knew each other on a more personal level. I did not give him any more detail. For the moment, JC and I wanted to spend time together and learn more about each other. Without prying eyes around us.

We discussed my salary for helping his father. CJ seemed happy his father would not be living alone anymore. The pay was meagre, but let's be honest, I was not there for the money. I wanted to be with my JC so we could sort out, together, what we would do with our lives. I would have stayed without the money.

CJ decided we needed a car, and it was done. (The other vehicle I had been using was from work; when I left, I needed to give it back.) With a car, we could adventure outside more, without having to pay a taxi. This made us both happy.

Life continued, ever-changing. Soon I could apply for a job that would provide me the opportunity to earn my NVQ3 certificate. This will be the first qualification I completed in English—the language I complained I would never be able to speak correctly.

I still had issues with my self-esteem. I thought I was not worth much. I thought I was old, tired, fat, and ugly. (The list in my head was much longer; full of negativities. I will not bore you with listing it all out.)

Anda was now working nights in a care home. I would have liked to work with her, but it was not the right place for me. I was looking for a place that was friendly, clean, with a kind, ambient environment. I went on some interviews, but none of them convinced me they were the right fit for me.

JC was still willing to help me find work. I was in a situation where I did not want to be more than a few hours without seeing him. Even when I went to the supermarket to do the shopping, I always looked forward to going back home to be with him. I was happy only if my eyes could catch sight of him. I was in love. Simple as that.

Anda had a pleasant surprise for me in May for my birthday. We went, for the day, to visit Waddesdon Manor, in Aylesbury, a city not far from my current home. I was a happy member of the National Trust. (National Trust is a conservation charity, protecting some of the UK's best-loved places.) The house was built in the Neo-Renaissance style of a French chateau, and it was full of surprises. The manor was astonishing, and the gardens were colourful and expansive. We had afternoon tea, with England's very famous scones, cream, and strawberry jam. I thoroughly enjoyed English afternoon tea.

JC waited at home, patiently. He did not want to go because he wanted a lazy day at home, without women. He wanted to stay in bed until late, and he did not want to run after us a place he had seen before. Or so he told me.

He had encouraged me, "Go and have a beautiful day. Chat in your fanny language. Feel free and enjoy this day." And before I left, he whispered in my ear to come back home soon—and safe.

127

English life in a small village suited me. I loved gardening, and I bought lots of flowers. I managed to mow the lawn. Both gardens, with their new plants and tidied yard, were full of colour and life.

JC came to check after I was done, and was very proud of my hard work. He told me to hire a gardener to do the hard work, but for me, it was not hard. I was happy doing it all by myself. Plus, Anda helped me with the yard work when she could.

I even had a new pair of boots for gardening after it rained. And, of course, I had my English raincoat.

I had never been so happy. Life was amazing!

In June, I had an interview for a job in a care home near Burford. The manager and the administrator were lovely. They had big smiles on their faces. I felt like I was taking tea with friends.

I took the job, and I was so excited about it. JC was not as happy, but he wanted me in a good mood. He understood my need for interaction with people, and for doing more than just keeping the house and gardening.

For two weeks, I worked during the day. After that, I worked nights.

Soon enough, I realised I was not very happy with my new job. After a month, all that seemed right was my salary. It was so lovely to have money.

My colleagues were nice for the most part. Yet some were very racist. There seemed to always be someone whose goal was to get others in trouble. I felt like I was walking in a minefield. You never knew what to expect. I quickly learned from others about what to do and who to trust. I also learned from my mistakes about the unwritten rules in a care home.

The men were all very nice, but some of my lady colleagues were real serpents. They were so polite and kind in front of you. The truth was far from that. The kindness these ladies showed, at first sight, was not their true nature. I discovered some were racist—hating foreigners. I told myself that in time, they would get to know me better, and they would love me. I was a hard worker, and I was not looking for trouble or problems. The good thing was all the foreigners banded together and helped each other.

I discovered shortly, amongst these ladies, there was a lovely one. She was a very calm, educated, and ladylike person—friendly, polite, and always understanding with everyone. It did not matter what country you came from; she appreciated a good worker, common sense, and intelligent conversation. She was adorable—my sweet Geraldine. I had lots of English friends, and the majority were beautiful people. Though I had the bad luck to work with some strange colleagues, Geraldine restored my faith in people. The manager, administrator, and secretary were also lovely people, sweet and gentile. Life seemed to sprinkle bad people in with the good ones.

Thank God I never felt racism in JC's village. People were so kind and friendly there. I never felt like an outsider. I always felt as if I was born there.

At home, JC knew everything about everything. He did not like my unhappiness at work. "You know you don't have to work. Stay at home. I am delighted with you here, my little 'foreigner.' I don't have any complaints. The house is so clean, your food is fantastic, the garden looks gorgeous, and I am happier than ever."

"Hahaha. I need to work if I want a pension. Bloody hell! Why are people so mean? Why aren't they all happy? Life is too short to be so delighted concocting things to make other people upset. The job is hard enough; you need to be kind, patient, and helpful to these older people. When the environment is full of bad energy around you, everything is harder."

"You can marry me, and you will have a pension, not to worry," JC informed me.

"I don't want to marry you for a pension," I chuckled.

"Okay, think of it. I hear you talk to your boyfriend from Italy. Doesn't seem to me you are happy at work. I know you are pleased around me," he continued.

Oh, he did not know how right he was. I was myself, laughing and peaceful, only near him. No problems, no worries, it was all so clear and bright. Thinking of life away from JC gave me pain in my stomach.

I sometimes talked to Matt. (That's who JC called my boyfriend from Italy.) Though I was sorry Matt was not happy without me, I realised more and more my place was here, near this unique Englishman.

There was a problem at work between me and a co-worker, Alina. Both of us were after a position in a unit we both liked and lies were told about me that could have cost me my career. I ended up being suspended for a month while an official investigation was conducted.

When I returned to work, cleared of any wrongdoing, I had to continue working with Alina. While I did not hate her, I still did not feel good about working with her.

The night manager, Amada, did not like the situation. The name Amada means 'love,' and the night manager lived up to her name—spreading love everywhere. She knew I was a nice person, just like she knew Alina did not like this situation—one that he created herself. I got the impression she was more concerned about Alina. They seemed to be good friends. They were always talking about something. She convinced me to forgive and forget.

Deciding I needed to address this issue myself, I talked to Alina, and after a while, I felt much better. I was angry because it was unfair to be accused of something you had not done. She was sorry. She had the impression I had done something wrong. But instead of talking to me about it, she went to the manager. I understood her motives were not entirely dark. She wanted the promotion, and in her mind, this was how she could get her competition out of the way. This is my personal opinion; it is what I concluded given what I knew about this story.

Talking to Amada was healing. Working with someone who had hurt me was a milestone for me. I must say Amada pushed me to discover something new about myself: I was capable of forgiveness.

I had started to work with Alina again, and even my husband was amazed that I did not hold a grudge against her. I liked what I felt at that moment. I had taken a huge step forward. Free of hate, I could concentrate on other things. I was happier at home and work. I started to see only what was positive in everything.

I also established a better relationship with the group of 'racist girls.' Maybe I only wanted to think about this positivity because I was happy.

⚜

JC invited me to eat out, and he asked the big question rightly, "We have been together now for two years. I am happy again. I must have done something right in my life to have this second chance at happiness. As a little boy, I used to be a singer in the church choir, maybe that's what I did right," he chuckled at his own joke. "I can see you are happy too, with me. I would be the most satisfied man in the word if you would marry me." He paused before continuing, "But, be careful, I won't ask again. I have asked you several times, but this is an official question. Would you like to be my wife?"

"YES! I will marry you. I am happy only near you," I answered. I knew from the bottom of my heart I wanted this.

"Tomorrow I will book a date for the marriage then," he stated matter-of-factly. His blue eyes glinted like the sea on a sunny day.

"Maybe you can call your son and talk about this," I suggested.

"No, I won't call him. I don't need a fuss."

"Oh God, I can't marry you as a thief, in hiding…"

JC stopped me. "He married the love of his life, has children, an excellent job, three servants—he has a wonderful life. I have done my best to help him get established. He will have the house…" he stopped. Reconsidering, he clarified, "Are you okay with this? That you won't have the house?"

"I don't care about the house. I don't want him to think I want only the property. But I still think it would be nice to tell him." I tried to encourage him to let his son know.

"Tell him if you want. I don't think he will be thrilled about having a stepmother. And a witch enchantress from the east! Hahaha!" This thought seemed to amuse him a lot. (In England, if you were an immigrant—Romanian, Polish, Hungarian, etc.—you were from the east. It was a way to call you a foreigner. And if you were a woman, you were a witch from the east.)

"JC, don't joke—this does not make me happy. I am not a witch from the east." Though it was supposed to be a joke, I felt really down thinking of his son hating me.

"You are a beautiful and intelligent witch. And I love you." His eyes still held a glimpse of irony, sweet-like…I did not hear anything more. My head was buzzing with the 'I love you' thing. It was the first time he told me this. It sounded so precious coming from him!

"Do you love me, then?" I asked him quietly, cautiously.

"I think this is love. It's love when you have butterflies in your stomach, isn't it?"

He was so cute, telling me I wanted to eat him with all his butterflies. (I meant that I would accept him no matter what.) We were laughing and trying to eat, but the food was awful. It had some strange dressings we did not like.

"It will be better to go home and have some real food. Your food is good. This is rubbish," JC finally said.

At home, we had 'real food.' The next day, JC booked our marriage for November, the first available date, in Oxford.

I called his son. I told him about all this. He asked me to let him get used to the idea of his father remarrying. I understood. When my father took another partner, I was not happy, initially. I still don't know if I would like my father to take another wife.

"Let him get used to it. I am marrying you the same in November. This is my last chance at happiness. He is a good boy; he will be happy for me, eventually," JC stated firmly.

We married in November. It was ugly and cold outside, but we were happy nonetheless. I had my sister, her husband, and Lydia present. Anda, of course, came along with some of my friends from Switzerland. JC was the best husband in the world. I was shining like a Christmas tree because it was all falling into place.

I was like dispersed pieces of a big jigsaw puzzle that were now put together, forming a beautiful landscape. Everything seemed positive and in peace with the universe.

At home, this ironic and serious man was a big child, happy every moment, laughing and playing, making me happy. Sometimes, when I was busy with the household chores, he hid in an empty room to scare me when he appeared in front of me.

One day, he told me to take a break because he wanted to talk to me. He actually tried pushing me into an armchair and said to enjoy some TV with him.

"You need to rest a bit. There is a show about history on the box, with Lucy Worsley. We like her. I can see you were raised in your country to work all the time, but in England, people enjoy a cuppa and an excellent TV show. You can do all these things in the house tomorrow. 'Domani,' as the Italians say, 'Domani.'"

I let everything wait—for him and Lucy Worsley. We adored her, and I thought she was the best English historian. No offence to others, but when she was talking, you could not move from the TV. The show explored the critical events of Henry VIII's six wives. With Lucy as a teacher, it was impossible to not love history.

JC and I loved a lot of the same things, and this was really helpful. I learned about World War II, history, ancient civilisations, and archaeology. Some interests, we did not share; I needed to be patient when he watched football or snooker. Hahaha. I did not like football, but I let him enjoy it.

I left the job I was at. For three months, I was at home, and JC was more pleased than ever.

Amada, my ex night manager, called me to meet her. We had dinner together, and she took me to her new place of work. It was an American chain of care homes. The place looked posh, clean, and inviting. Only one unit was open; it smelled new and unused. I thought, *"I would like to work here."*

CHAPTER 8

I Am Getting There

Home, home, home! This word was like music to my ears. For me, the word 'home' had a new significance. Home was anywhere near my sweet husband. He was my world and the centre of my life. I did everything possible to see that beautiful smile on his face. Every week, when it was not raining, we took the car and visited various places. JC liked to walk near the rivers, and stop at a pub for a pint after.

For longer trips, I went with Anda and used our National Trust membership. Every month, we tried to see something new around the area, like gardens, castles, manors, or Roman villas. Before going home, we liked to have English tea at whatever place we were visiting. Once back at home, my love was thrilled to see me again, always in a good mood.

I felt so much love; something I never thought could be possible. Earlier in my life, when I was dreaming about days like these, I was sure they would only be dreams. They would never come to fruition.

Now, this is not the case. There were rarely days I was upset, or worrying about something, or arguing. In fact, JC did not want or know how to argue. When I came back from work tired and angry about some problem, he applied his medicine—kindness and love.

"Come here near me, and tell me why you are sad," he would say. Then he opened his massive arms, held me on his knees, and caressed me, all with a big smile on his beautiful face.

After he found out 'the big problem' that bothered me, he would hug me with tenderness.

"And this is 'the big problem?' Hahaha. You don't have problems, my love. If you 'think' there is a problem, there is something simple to be done about it: eliminate the problem. From your mind, from your cares."

"What does it mean, 'eliminate the problem?'" I asked. "It is impossible to kill some awful colleagues."

"That is true. But, if you don't like the job, quit it. Simple as that. The problem is gone. Poof! Gone. If you don't want to talk on the phone to someone, cancel the number, and poof. If you don't want someone to bother you, walk away, and poof!"

"You think it's simple like that? I can't eliminate all these things; I will be alone. Sometimes we need to be kind, even with people we don't like. If we tell others all we feel, we will hurt them." I explained.

"Who said this? You are intelligent, but you are complicating your life. Keep only friends near you, and let go of the 'energy vampires.' You must love yourself to the point that you eliminate what is bothering you. Quit this bloody job; you will find better a better one. You create your life. Be careful, nothing up and nothing down…try to do the best of your life, now, not 'domani.' You are very unhappy at work; I can see it. I want to see you happy. Quit and look for better things."

I quit that job.

For three months, I was at home, and JC was more pleased than ever. In my mind, not being employed is a disaster. JC was making me lazy. He told me it was making me more relaxed and healthier. After a month, I got his point. I had no more headaches or stress, and no more hurtful people to avoid. My life was filled with love, peace and quiet, and laughter.

Author's note: "Nothing up and nothing down" was JC's favourite phrase. He meant there were no angels and no demons. And there was no heaven or hell or afterlife. Life was what it was, and what mattered was here and now.

I talked on the phone every three or four days to my father. He was amazed by how happy I was. I supposed he was the only one in my family to be pleased that I married an older man.

"My soul is at peace, my love, when I talk to you because I feel all your happiness. I have never heard you like this, and I am so grateful to your husband for this. I would like to know him and tell him thank you for your laughter and joy," he told me.

If I didn't call him, he called me. He must have missed me. I missed him, too. I would have liked to see him, but I was not very keen on leaving JC alone. He would be swamped with newspapers and TV, and he would always be hungry.

My friend from Italy, Carmella, suggested I go spend some time with Dad that summer. She would come to my house and take care of my husband. She visited us the previous Christmas. She knew JC, and she was an exceptional cook, as well. As a teacher, she would have an extended annual leave in the summer. I could choose when to go for a week to see Dad.

"Take a week for your father; you never know what will happen. Our parents are old now; you will be sorry if you don't go when you are still in time. I promise JC will be okay. He will be still here in a week, but your father is getting worse day by day, and you will be sorry if you don't go see him. And for me, it will be a relaxing holiday, you know I love England and your house," Carmella explained.

I knew I was lucky she could do this for me. Anda could not miss a day at work; the same with my other friend, Elena. They helped when they could, but it was not always possible. I was grateful to them for all the help they gave me, but I could not ask more. Carmella was a lot of help, and she knew I always paid my debts.

JC and I agreed I would go for a week in August to visit Dad, while he would have Carmella help at the house.

He tried arguing at first, "I don't need a babysitter, but if you are happier with her being here, I will try to be kind to her. I think she likes England. And you need someone to water your flowers. Hahaha! I won't need to worry about them." He was always joking, but it was good he accepted the help.

JC knew my feelings about Dad and was pleased to see I was making a step in this direction. Sometimes, when I was talking on the phone to my father, I realised he had been drinking, and my facial expression changed. I became sad. He was not drunk, but he was in that exciting mood which made him talk a lot and gave him some dramatic shadows in the way he expressed himself. I knew he was on medication for heart and was not supposed to drink. I did not say anything, but I was upset. His partner knew he could not drink, as well. I wondered what she was doing about it? I knew how hard it was to fight with him, but…

JC would try to make me feel better. "Love, there is nothing you can do about this. You are here, try to be happy. Don't over-think your father's problem. It is pointless. If we can help send him somewhere for professional help, then let them help him."

"Thanks, JC, it is so kind of you. He would never go. I am worried about him because I am aware of what happens when you mix medicines and alcohol."

"At this moment, you cannot do anything. Calm down. Think positive."

"How?" I asked him desperately.

"What is the only thing you have power over?" He asked me.

"Sorry? I do not have power over anything. I have never had..." I started.

"Wrong. You are the only one in the entire world to have power over your thoughts. What do you choose to think at this moment? Your thoughts are up to you and you alone. Nobody else can decide—not me, not friends, not family, not even God—only you. Take mental control, quiet the chatter in your head, and use the mind as a tool for pleasant thoughts. You cannot change things related to your father, but you can have a definite vision about your life in the present. You are married to me, a handsome and intelligent man," he laughed. "You have a beautiful life, good friends, and a delightful garden."

"How can I think positive when problems are shouting in my head?"

"Love, if there is a problem, you have two possibilities: one, if the problem can be solved, solve it and don't worry, and two, if you can't do something about it, let it go. Why worry either way? You can't do anything about your Dad, so let go."

"Okay, okay. For you everything is so easy," I said a bit sarcastically.

"Is not easy, but no one can tell us to feel bad or not. You can choose to think about problems or not. If you want to be happy, quiet your mind, and tell it you've decided to be positive and content—the master of your own mind. Your father has the problem, not you. You cannot make yourself miserable about his choices.

"My father was an electrical engineer, sent to work around the world when the British Empire built new aero ports. He was on his own most of the time and used to drink—lots. I hated him for years. Until I understood this hatred was poisoning my soul. There was no way he could be helped unless he wanted help. I did not expect anything from him after that. Instead, I concentrated on myself and the rest of the family. I said to myself,

'I forgive him and bless him,' but I let his problems go. Most of all, I excused myself for all the evil thoughts I had for him. He had done what he could. He did not know he could do better. It was up to me to keep thinking, hating, or to let go…I choose to be happy and build a beautiful life for myself.

"Forgiveness can be hard to achieve, but it is so healing. After all, he created a good and creative bloke like me.

"My love, try to be brave, and you will always be happy and content. Even in a pleasant atmosphere, the weak person remains half-hearted. You can choose what you want to be." JC explained this all to me.

I understood. "You're right, love, as usual. I don't want you to worry about my lousy thoughts. It's all fine. You are a treasure, this is the truth," I told my marvellous maestro.

"Go for a walk, you'll feel better."

"It is raining…"

"When on the Earth the rain stopped someone from getting out? We have boots and raincoats in England."

"Yes, Master JC, I have all this." I went for a nice walk—after five minutes in the rain, it was sunny again, and I felt better.

On my walk, many thoughts ran through my head. What are human beings without hope? Nothing. Even when you were worried about your small, miserable problems, there was hope things would get better. Hope for a new, beautiful day; hope for a better life; hope for an excellent mark on an exam; hope for a better job; hope to be loved; hope for healing when we have an illness; hope our children and loved ones will be protected and happy. The point being that hope remained.

One hour later, my thoughts cleared. JC was right. I worried about everything, including a bit of rain. With hope in my heart, I walked the road back to my love, at home. I felt better.

I thought about Dad. He was in a good mood, happy for me, but I felt sad about his drinking.

Once, on the phone, he told me he had leukaemia. My heart hit my chest furiously, and I could not talk at first. Once I could, I tried my best to assure him he was a strong man and would be fine.

It was the first time I felt his fear—fear of death. And the first time I realised, for him this was the beginning of his end.

There were also heart problems. I did not want him to drink at all with all these diseases. I wanted my father alive for years and years to come.

I lived with the hope that God would help him to realise what he needed to do to heal himself, or at least extend what was left.

I accepted Amada's proposal, and I applied for a job where she was employed as the night manager.

Things were all right, in the beginning, with only a unit opened. However, within a few months, all four units of the building were populated with residents. There was more staff, too, though not enough. Problems were starting. We felt we were short-staffed, but management saw things differently.

The work was hard. Some colleagues were quite mean, making everything harder.

I made a friend, Alida, a beautiful Hungarian woman. She was a nurse, but she was awaiting her nurse-pin, so she took work as a senior carer, like me. I got along fine with her, but she had trouble with other colleagues. This was no surprise to me. She was a tough-skinned person who said what she thought. Some people found it hard to digest the truth.

As soon as she completed her language test, she went to a hospital to work as a nurse, and I was short a friend at work.

Amada left the job as well; she moved within the same company to another home, as a night manager. I would have liked to continue to walk with her, but her new job was too far from my house. I was heartbroken.

We had a new night manager, a young nurse—Romanian—John. I was happy with the new manager; with Amada gone, it had been somewhat tough. I was impressed by how professional he was and how much heart he put into his work. I had a new colleague too, Johana, who was Romanian as well. She came from the same region as John. It was always a pleasure to work with them.

I thought they would make a perfect couple. They worked together in harmony; that was rare at this job. There was no need to tell one to another what to do; they just completed each other's thoughts, and the work flowed. It was like watching two ballet dancers on stage moving with precision acquired after years of hard work together. The only thing is they were natural together, nobody had taught them how to dance.

I was amazed because both were doing lots of extra work—things they did not have to do—but they did it with pleasure. They would be a wonderful couple, but it seemed they did not see this. They liked each other, I could feel it, but they let this beautiful chance disappear. I thought young people were so stupid sometimes. They had a rare gem in front of them, and they turned their back, running after stones in the street. Maybe they were frightened or overwhelmed. Perhaps they both thought they were too beautiful to be faithful.

This workplace was becoming a mess. I was growing tired of it. I was still there because of John and Johana, but they seemed tired too.

The manager was a nice person but did not understand the pressure we felt, and what working nights meant to us.

JC laughed again when I explained my workplace problems to him, yet again.

He was still adamant. "You don't have problems, my love. You are free to choose. Leave the job."

Everything was simple for my love.

I chose to keep going because I did not think it was good to jump from job to job. At this point, I was only working two nights per week.

JC told me I needed to love myself more. Maybe he was right, but I kept fighting, hoping something would change. I was sure all these places were the same; the problems were everywhere. And here again, I showed my desire to fix things, to show myself I could do it.

Was it possible to love myself more? And how? By changing jobs?

I was so lucky to have peace at home. This was priceless. Maybe it was impossible to have it all. Perhaps I had to pay, somehow, for the happiness I had with JC.

Because of the stress at work, I put on weight, so I started to go swimming, for exercise. I got up at six in the morning and swam from seven to eight. Once at home, I was tired, but I continued with half an hour running on the treadmill, watching something on the box.

JC watched me one day, and moved his head, talking to himself. He had one eye on the TV and one eye on me. Suddenly, he asked, "Why are you killing yourself like this?"

I responded, panting, "I am fat, and I don't like myself."

"Hmmm, and you think all this exercise is helping? Isn't it better if you cut things from your menu like ice cream, bread, and butter—if you eat less?"

Now I became distraught. Did JC think I ate too much? So, I asked him, "Do you think I am fat because I eat too much ice cream?"

"You are not fat! Do you understand that? At 20 we are skinny, but at 40 our bodies change. Don't hope to look like models; you are beautiful and healthy, pneumatic, and I love how you look."

I was not listening. "Okay, I will renounce ice cream."

JC sighed. "You don't need to kill yourself with all these exercises. Eat less junk and more healthy food—that will help you. You need to love yourself more. And stop with the rubbish the TV is putting in your head. You are working a lot around the house and garden; just cut out sugary and fatty foods."

I started to cook more vegetables, and I forfeited my daily cup of frozen delight. JC sniggered at me when we were at the table, but I knew he loved me and wanted me to be happy, at peace with myself. He was tall and thin; he had an outstanding figure. But I must say he supported me by eating very slowly, being careful to put away the fatty parts of food, and drinking his beverages unsweetened. At the same time, he was eating lots of Italian chocolate, but did not put weight on. I was jealous he could do this.

Work continued to be a nightmare. I was happy when working with John, Johana, and Amelia, another friend. We did our jobs and tried to make our shift more comfortable by laughing and eating together. I was sure other colleagues were not impressed by this, but we did not care too much. It was impossible to make all of them happy.

John worked all night, with the eyes on Johana. Sometimes, he did not hear me when I asked something, I felt soon they would be together.

One night, Johana looked upset about something. She was doing the job quietly, which was unusual for such a high-spirited girl. She was always laughing.

John came in from the kitchen, and once in front of Johana, he put something in her hand.

"What is this? Why are you giving me a potato?" she angrily asked.

"It is a potato, but it is in a heart shape," he answered genuinely.

She did not change her mood. And she seemed to not appreciate the heart-potato.

I wanted to do something to help them, but I did not know what to do. I did not want to interfere, even though I would have liked, with all my heart, to 'fix' them. I would have been happy to see them together, enjoying their lives as a couple. I talked to Amelia, and she thought the same thing—they loved each other but were both stupid.

JC laughed again at my work as Cupid. "Let people in peace! Don't be Cupid because you could get into trouble."

"That is the problem, maybe I need to do something about it, talk to them," I insisted.

"Stop trying to fix other people's lives. I know you are happy, and you want everybody to feel the same way, but it is impossible. They will be fine.

"Come here and make me a nice cup of strawberries with ice cream, since you don't eat it. I don't want that container in the freezer to get lost," he teased while sending me the best smile that he could get on his beautiful face. I did not want him to eat *my* ice cream, but I chose not to eat it. I would get fat. Ufff!

After my chat with JC about forgiveness, I changed a bit day by day. In a few months, I felt different. I did not think about my arguing with Dad anymore; I concentrated on having a friendly relationship with him. Every day that passed, my chats with Dad went better and better. He could not wait to see me; every call,

147

he asked how many days were left until I came. I had a warm feeling, thinking he was waiting for my arrival.

Summer finally arrived. I was going to visit my father for one week. I worried a bit we would argue, again, about something, even if everything had seemed fine lately.

Carmella was coming to England as promised. I was happy I would be able to see JC through her WhatsApp. JC did not like phones. He never had one near, and I would feel lost not knowing how he was.

Once at my father's house, I was very busy with work in the main house. My sister had done a significant job maintaining it in the past—15 years ago—but now the house needs some more improvement.

In the same courtyard as the house, there was another set of buildings. There was a barn-like building where hay was stored in the loft for the animals. On one side of this barn, there was a shelter for animals. On the other side was a small cottage/summer house. It did not have a washroom in it as it was intended for temporary use only. Various jobs would be done in this area. For example, when Mom was cooking fish, she would cook it in this summer house—to keep the smell out of the house.

Dad and his partner, Eva, were living in this small cottage. My sister and I decided to help them to move into a bigger house. Dad was getting older, and he needed to have a place in better condition to keep him in good health. He appeared happy to do it, but he worried about the cost.

We had a busy but happy week. It was the first time we enjoyed everything about the visit.

I noticed Dad was not as healthy as he was years ago. He appeared to have more difficulties hearing and was slow at processing discussions. Sometimes he looked absent, and Eva told me he no longer understood everything going on around him. Because of this, he did not participate too much anymore. He was in the cottage more lately, watching TV, but he would get angry every time he needed to change the channel because he could not remember how. I recognized these signs as I was working in a care home. Maybe he had Alzheimer's or something like that.

I looked at this still handsome old man. I felt as though I had stones on my chest because of the pain I felt. He would become more and more frustrated as he forgot more things. He was always curious about everything—reading a lot and teaching people around him. Now he seemed lost most of the time. He was also very quiet. His eyes were full of life when I was near him. He was lucid for a moment, and we talked about things he wanted only me to hear. For most of the day, he slept or watched TV, lost in his world. Sometimes I could hear him arguing with Eva. She seemed tired of him and of repeating things when he did not understand. I wondered what would happen when he got worse. Mom would have approached the situation with love, as she had always done. But things were different now.

After eight days, the house was almost ready, and I needed to let Eva finish the job. I could not stay more, I had a flight to take, and my JC was waiting for me. For how much I loved to be near Dad, I missed my husband—his eyes, his smile, and his warmth. I missed our talking and his kisses, his velvety voice telling me all would be fine, to not worry about things, because he was there.

Dad did not understand why I could not stay longer, and this did not help me. I had the feeling this was the last time I would see him. My stomach seemed to be in my mouth; I wanted to cry. It was a pain to leave him, and a pain to stay. Every cell of my body was shouting and hurting, confusing me more. I wanted to be near my father to help him more. Yet I wanted to be near JC. I was laughing in front of my father, but once in bed, I cried. I would be so happy if Mom were still here to support him.

I found myself at peace when back in my JC's arms. He wanted to know everything; he was thrilled to see me back home. Before going to Romania to visit, JC told me to congratulate Dad for the way he educated and raised his daughter, aka me. I told my father this when I was there, and he started to cry.

"Did you told your father what I said? He needed to know it," JC asked when I returned.

"Yes, love. He cried. He sent lots of love. He was happy for us," I told JC.

"Good. I was worried your father would be upset because you married an old man," he jested.

"No worries. It was the first time when we didn't argue, and we had a wonderful time together," I reminisced.

"I hope you feel better now. Now go to the kitchen and get me something good to eat. I was starving with your friend here." He looked so severe, I believed him for a moment. Then I caught that glimpse in his eyes, and I knew he was joking. He was glad to have me back, he just wanted something made by my hands so he could feel the normality of our lives again. He ate what Carmella had made him, at least it seemed so from the photos she sent to me. Thank God she was intelligent and understood his sense of humour.

My holidays were finished, so I returned to my job. Nothing changed. We were still short-staffed, and there was still lots of stress. I went only because of my friends. At home, with my love, was the place where I felt happy. I was not religious, but

I found myself thanking God for all I had, and most of all, for my husband.

God bless this man for his love and kindness. For his patience, teaching, and calmness.

CHAPTER 9

Life Lessons

Even with an exhausting job, I felt blessed—touched by love and happiness. JC changed my life. I now had an excellent relationship with Dad. I was positive and constructive with my friends. And I was more willing to help without expecting something on exchange. It seemed positive thinking brought stability and love into my life. Sometimes I wanted to go outside and shout, "I AM HAPPY!"

Mornings were the best part of my days now. Once my eyes were opened, I felt blessed about everything around me. Even the spider near the chandelier that insisted on building its web there despite my everyday cleaning.

My morning routine started with covering my husband's face in kisses until he complained to stop it or to not overdo it. I would kiss him a thousand times until he started to play fight with me, playing the fed up one. His eyes told me another thing; they were pleased and full of happiness and love.

Love, love, love…a word with such a power. In our modern days, the word 'love' appears to have people in total confusion.

There is a lot of talk about the word, but the more we talk, the more we contradict ourselves. It is so complicated, or do we make it more difficult than it is? I am sure if you ask 10 of your friends about love, they will all respond differently, pushing you to frustration. I have inquired with my friends, and they see love as empathy, partnership, sex, devotion, security, comfort, serenity, suffering, passion, commitment, fulfilment, etc. They are all confused about the word; none of them can define it with clarity, like in a dictionary. The things everybody seems to want, for themselves, include fewer obstacles, less drama, more patience, and mutual support.

Ancient Greeks used different words to distinguish among the ways of experiencing what we call, simply, 'love.' They indicate there are different kinds of love, calling them philia=>friend bond, storge=>familiar love, pragma=>enduring love, mania=>obsessive love, philautia=>self-love, eros=>romantic love, agape=>unconditional love, and ludus=>playful love. There may be more, but the idea is they were smart, and they tried to put their thoughts to peace instead of spending too much thinking about love. They believed every one of these kinds of love gave you something; they all had truth and beauty. But separately, I think, they all were missing something only one other had to offer. The sum of the parts was never equal to the individual parts. Were they so bright, after all, these Greeks? Are you happy only with eros or storge or agape? At some point or another, I bet you will want something more, or something different altogether.

Growing up, we likely experienced storge and philia, love for our families and friends. Later we probably dreamt about eros and agape, having both if lucky enough. Looking back on my relationships with men, I can now see clearly how much I had prioritised eros. I focussed energy on pain and suffering, thinking love meant harder obstacles to overcome. I have always tried to fix things, wanted to heal someone, or to show my love was something special that would provide a return. The result was I ended up hurt and disappointed. I thought I was not good enough, I did not deserve things, or I was not worthy of being loved. My self-thoughts got in my way.

That was my point of view about myself. Now I can see how wrong I was. It is called 'point of view' for a reason, no? It is just a 'point,' in time or space—nothing else. If you lay on the beach, keeping your back to the sea with a view of only people and buildings in front of you, life appears as an anteater, noisy and tiring—a very busy place. This is one 'point of view.' But if you lay on the beach, facing the sea, in front of you is a blue, peaceful, infinite blanket of water, and life appears relaxed and happy. Your point of view depends on what you choose to see and how you choose to see it.

Media these days teaches us romantic love (eros) must contain suffering and passion in order to bring us to fulfilment. Here, the problem starts. Men and women break up in disappointment and frustration. The truth is we are most happy when a relationship flows without headaches, dramas, or yearnings.

What I was living near my JC, love was a mixture of philia, mania, eros, and agape. All my energy was focussed on him. I knew I was obsessed with him being happy, comfortable, loved, and cared for. Some of this was because I knew we didn't have a lot of time, like couples who met earlier in life had. He was much older than me, and we both were living each day as if the next would never come. We had respect, mutual trust, devotion, understanding, and the willingness to support each other. We tolerated our differences. He pushed me to be creative, to grow as an individual, and to express myself without fear.

My husband wanted me happy. That included being surrounded by friends. When I was invited out for a birthday or a girl's evening, he insisted I go. I didn't want to upset him, so I would go, but I was not happy more than a few hours away from him. I knew he wanted to have a 'normal' life. He didn't want to think of death, how short a time we might have together, or anything like that. Once I came home, he would ask me if I enjoyed the time spent with friends. I would answer positively, making him happy, as if he had done something great for me. But, in truth, I was in peace only when I was near him, in a place where I could lay my eyes on him.

I mentioned before that JC made me lazy. I still think of it because after dinner he wouldn't let me do the washing up. He insisted on relaxing and doing the dishes in the morning. I wanted everything clean in the kitchen after dinner, but he always won. We watched TV instead, or we talked. Sometimes I merely relaxed in my armchair, near him, exploring YouTube.

One day I came across Craig Hamilton's YouTube channel and the book he wrote, <u>Mystic Journey to India</u>. The book is about his journey to India where he stumbled upon a 5,000-year-old Indian prophecy, a future story told by an Oracle, with his name on it. This prophecy had him perform strange rituals, cleanse his life, and change people's lives through charitable acts. It was an interesting story; I wondered what this prophecy could tell me.

For the moment, a trip to India was outside of my plans. Still, I became more curious about mindfulness, yoga, and meditation. I also felt drawn to new discoveries about the ancient world.

When I had spare time, I explored YouTube. I was excited because you could find audiobooks, which were easy for me to listen to while cooking or cleaning the house, or even gardening.

There were lots of annoying adverts every five minutes, and I hated these interruptions. Usually, I would let the ad run for three seconds, then skip the annoying thing, but for some reason, I let a full ad run one day.

A beautiful woman was talking about her online business. One that allowed her to work from anywhere in the world that had an internet connection and a laptop. In the ad, she was in a woodhouse, near the sea, surrounded by palms and stunning beaches. She appeared tanned and happy. Her name was Karolina, and from her accent, she wasn't English. In fact, she didn't even speak English correctly. I must say this woman, who appeared for four minutes in this advert, changed my future. This would also impact JC. I'm sure it will also affect other people to come.

I subscribed to her emails, and I understood it was about affiliate marketing education. This online Marketing Academy taught members a variety of ways to sell products or services, anywhere in the world; how to build an Internet marketing business from scratch; and it provided the support and training necessary for you to achieve your goals.

I started this adventure, doing all the online courses, participating in all the webinars. I was thrilled. The Facebook community was impressive. I made lots of friends, and I discovered the importance of helping others. I learned about 'The Law of Attraction.' This New Thought philosophy is the belief that the way you think will bring back positive or negative experiences in your life. Seems like this law is the magnetic power of the Universe. It is like gravity in the way it attracts people, thoughts, and circumstances to you.

This powerful Law of Attraction enthralled me. Imagine if this was a topic in the schools. Millions of children could learn how to spread kindness, compassion, love, and positivity, and how to get back from the Universe the same things. Wouldn't life be more comfortable and beautiful? Working to maintain a high frequency by projecting positive thoughts, you inevitably end up with more positive things in your life. Who wouldn't want this?

Often in life, it is difficult to be happy because our neighbour or friend has more than us—a better car, house, job, or life. We might be jealous of another person's helpful family or because our friends' children are better at school? We are living in continuous competition with others; we are unhappy; we want more and more.

All of this starts with our thoughts. Instead of being unhappy with what we don't have, we should be happy about what we do have.

Once, my JC said to me that the only thing in the world we had power over was our thoughts. We could choose how to start the day, even with the worst conditions in place. It should be enough to open the window and give a look to your garden (if you are lucky enough to have one). Or to appreciate your spouse or children. Or to appreciate your dog, cat, or fish. Or even to say to yourself you are grateful for another day on Earth. You need to find something positive to think about, no matter how bad you may think your situation is. Someone, somewhere, would be happy to be where you are today.

I am sure, as scholars, you had a day when the beautiful weather or friends attracted you to play instead of doing your homework. You may have chosen to go out to play, but the film playing in your head about the next day at school was making you crazy. You may have thought and rethought about what would happen the next day when the teacher pointed at you to answer, and you'd be in trouble. You might spend hours broadcasting your film in your head; you might not sleep most of the night, and then guess what, the next day plays out exactly how you thought it would.

Maybe you are going to an interview, you may even be the best person for the job, but you are not hired. You may have been frightened in the meeting. You may have told yourself you were not good enough for the job. You may wonder why they would choose you where there are lots of other people vying for the same position. Blah, blah, blah! If you appear in front of the interviewer, like a frightened rabbit in front of the hunter, you'll be declined for sure. But if you are going confident, telling yourself you are the best choice for the job, you'll be appreciated, respected, and maybe you'll get the position.

The Law of Attraction was a small part of my course at the academy I subscribed to, but I thought it was the best thing I ever had learned. I didn't know yet how this would help me with my online business, but I was in love with the concept.

For one of my assignments, I had to watch a film, 'The Shift.' It was the first time I heard or saw Wayne Dyer. I felt blessed; I would have liked to know him and have a chat. I watched it a couple of times; it had a fantastic life lesson. His calm voice was music to my ears. The message was simple, yet it gave you lots to think about. The premise was to do things that made you happy—something you only dreamt about—without fear of being approved or not. I suggest checking out the Wayne Dyer channel on YouTube; you'll find a myriad of videos to help you gain knowledge and peace for your mind.

I decided to go to a meditation webinar, but I was late. I caught only the last 15 minutes of the session. The video showed a woman sitting quietly in an armchair with her eyes closed. Strange music played in the background. Nothing changed until the last minute when she opened her brown eyes and thanked the participants for their presence. I was baffled. I wanted to be present at the beginning of the next session. All this talk about meditation, and that was all it was? It couldn't be true.

After 10 lessons, I knew much more. Meditation would become my morning routine. I found Abraham Hicks on YouTube. His video, 'Things Are Always Working Out for Me,' became my morning prayer. (It is a meditation to start your day with a positive mind.) This routine gave me positive energy and positive energy was so important in order to start a good day. Of course, that was to be combined with my JC's presence. He was more important than anything else. Without him and my meditation, I think I would be a pale shadow of what I am today.

I saw Anda less and less because of her work. I missed our talks, our trips with National Trust, and our cigarettes in the garden. JC missed her too and asked from time to time about her.

I made an excellent new friend, Elena, who was 10 years younger than me. I met her at my previous job. She was working with us, coming from an agency, and we became friends shortly after that. She was the kind of person everyone would like to have as a friend. When I went to London on a course for two days, she cooked for my husband and took care of the house. I put money in her account because she renounced (called in sick) a day with her agency. She would not accept it; I had it back within minutes. She told me she did it as a friend, and that she did not need to be paid for it. I always managed to pay my debts, but with her, I never won. She accepted only some little presents for her daughter, Adriana. But she kept visiting me, bringing a box of chocolates, flowers, or food. She was always smiling, happy, and positive. She was good company for me.

JC still tried to make me leave my job. After my shifts, I was sad and tired, even though I was happy to work with John and Johana. Even some of the residents kept me there because they were so glad to see me. I knew I was doing something good for them.

Meditation helped me develop a new approach to things I didn't like. I needed to be thankful for the job, the staff, and the residents. Then I needed to let the negativity go, leaving myself open to a better job, one that would give me more satisfaction. I was testing this Law of Attraction.

Christmas arrived again, and I was still in the same place, in the same conditions, only I was much more tired.

Home was paramount. I was in seventh heaven. JC decided, as usual, on our Christmas menu.

In the last two weeks, I developed problems with my left hand. It was difficult even to drive, and I had to wear a rigid support. The doctor said it was Carpal Tunnel Syndrome, and I was to restrict any manual handling at work. JC would cook under my supervision, everything for Christmas. He would even bake the walnut cake we loved so much. He was enthusiastic about helping me, being the boss, for once, in the kitchen.

I managed to wash and peel some veggies while JC prepared the turkey. He insisted on having one, but I did not know who would eat all this food. Anda used to spend Christmas with us, but this year she would be working. I found the smallest turkey I could, but it would still be too big for us.

It was so lovely to see JC as the kitchen king. He was so posh in everything he did. Now, among veggies, meat, and pots and pans, he looked like a researcher doing something of national importance. This was ironic to me because he worked as a researcher during his working days.

I set all the ingredients for the cake in front of him. He was even better at preparing them than me. I was amazed. The sponge was soon ready; I put it under a tea towel to rest. Then he made the cream, and I put my fingers in it, checking every second. He took some cream with the spoon, and he flung it on my face. I was not expecting this. For a moment I couldn't believe it. I wanted to do the same to him, but he ran around the kitchen table, and it was impossible to put my hands on him. He was laughing, asking me to stop, but I did not listen. He started it, now he wanted me to stop? He kept the bowl with the cream in his hands, and I noticed a pack of white flour. I picked some up and threw it at him. JC was now a snowman, laughing like a child, begging me to stop.

It was the best Christmas ever!

It took several hours to clean up everything with only one hand, but we were still laughing and teasing each other. I asked JC to make the syrup to wet the cake, but he had a better idea. Baileys liqueur seemed to be the right choice, and he sprinkled the cake with it. I was worried it would be a mistake, but his cake was the best walnut cake ever. We spent all day together, no visitors, and I went to work that evening in an excellent mood. I worked happily, knowing the morning would come and I could go home to be near my love, happy to see his beautiful face again.

At work, Johana was acting strangely. I could not resist, and I found the courage to ask about John and her. She opened up a bit, and I found out he had a girlfriend back in Romania. He thought it was better to talk to her, to free himself, and start a clean, new relationship with Johana after New Year. He was at home for Christmas. She was patient, but she had a bad feeling about this. I thought she was young—only 22 years old—she had to suffer a bit for love. John was the right person for her, and I hoped the next year would bring happiness for both of them. I was so happy, and I wanted all my friends to feel the same.

But life was full of surprises. When John came back, the Universe decided something else for them. Something happened, and they could not meet to talk.

On Sunday morning, John went to church, and Johana disappeared from his mind. The next week, working with him, I found out he met a woman, and he was in love with her. He was excited because she was a beautiful woman, and most of all, a good girl, who attended church.

I was mute. I tried to appear happy for him. I had the feeling that in some time, he would wake up. He would realise this wouldn't work. He told Johana about the other woman. She acted normal, but I wondered where this young woman found all her toughness. I was near her and knew she missed her mother, especially at that moment. I talked to her, kept her busy, and gave her some motherly cuddles when she was sad. She didn't talk about John. She tried to be the same good friend to him, but she threw herself on food.

"Stop fixing people! They are young, they will sort out their problems," JC said to me when I told him about all this. He was trying to make me smile. He didn't want me sad, so he took me in his warm arms, and I forgot all about my friends' problems. I was always over the moon near my love. He had a good story every time I needed to change my bad mood. In these four years together, I laughed every single day. Was I just lucky, or was there an unknown force in the Universe, guiding things in a certain way? I thought for a long time that I didn't deserve happiness in my life, and I would never have it. And here I was, with five-star love surrounding me, no tears, no pain, no drama.

"I must have done something right in my life to deserve this!" My beautiful JC used to say every day, in the morning, when I kissed him. I felt the same way.

In March, my friends, Anita and Carla, organised a night out, dinner and dancing somewhere. JC insisted, again, that I go. I thought it would be nice to see the girls and do something different. Elena came with us. We had dinner in Carla's town, and after we went to a Portuguese club. The girls were enjoying dancing again, like teenagers, and they didn't stop for hours. After one cocktail, I was done; I wanted to go home. I sat there watching my friends, listening to good music, but I wanted to be near my love. I was happy when in bed, in my husband's arms—this was truly music to my ears.

At the end of March, my husband became unwell. He developed a rash on his lower left back; it appeared as red blotches on his skin. I thought he had a fall on the stairs, maybe during the night, when I was at work. I felt guilty. I called the medical centre for an appointment, but they were busy; I could not get into the place until the next day.

The previous month, Anda was very ill, and she went to Oxford, to a private centre. In England, there is two-tier health care. The public system—which was free to use—would force people to wait months for an appointment. The private system, which cost money, would allow people access to the doctors quicker. I booked an appointment for the next day at the same private centre Anda has used, but JC was very upset. He refused to go, saying he was in significant pain and didn't feel well. There was no way to convince him to go, and I was almost crying. The previous week he didn't eat enough, so now I started to worry.

I sent a photo of the blotches to the doctor. The doctor responded the rash was shingles. I googled this word, and I was petrified. JC needed to see a doctor. I was lucky enough to convince someone at the medical centre to send a specialist to see him at home. Now his blotches were blisters, oozing fluid, and itchy. He could not even lie on his left side. I was happy he got medicine. For almost two weeks, he had to take medication. Still, his back got worse, and now the rash moved to his front, only this time on the left side of the genitals. Ouch!

My man who had never complained about pain was now as a little child. I could not even touch the bed. When I gave him a wash in bed, it was a nightmare for both of us. He had tears in his blue eyes, and I had tears because I didn't want him to suffer so much.

"Oh, God, please take all this pain from him and give it to me," I prayed with all my soul. But God seemed to be very busy these days; He never answered me.

This was April.

John and Johana gave their resignations at work. With JC in this situation, I did the same. I needed to be near my loved one every second; he was the most important thing in my life. I felt overwhelmed about this illness. I had a bad feeling. I felt heartbroken, crying about nothing. Most of all, I was frightened because of his lack of eating.

"My love, why don't you eat? Is your throat hurting? Would you like anything else? Just tell me what you prefer, please," I pleaded with JC.

"Don't worry, I'll be fine, you'll see. I will eat, okay? You are worrying too much. I am happy. I don't want to die now. I'll be fine. Don't fuss so much," he responded as he took me in his arms. I was crying, and he did not like it.

Within four weeks, I called for the paramedics to see him at home five times. I talked to his son. He cheered me up a bit by telling me he had shingles too. He suffered a lot, but it was something that healed. Thanks to him, I had hope that JC would be okay in a couple of weeks.

This hope fell apart shortly. I had an emptiness in my chest. JC wouldn't eat much—some strawberries, ice cream, a boiled egg. If I was lucky, some chicken soup. I ground meat and made him a cream soup, but he would only have a few spoonfuls.

The day before my 49th birthday in late May, I called the paramedics again. I was shaking all over. The paramedic sent JC to the hospital. He needed vitamins and hydration. He was drinking Lucozade, but it wasn't enough. I was with him at the hospital. I felt happier as I knew he would receive the help he needed. Maybe they would make him eat.

There were two young doctors there; they were patient and wonderful, checking on him for hours. Now I could smile when holding my husband's arm. He was quiet, joking with these two young specialists, telling them he wanted to live, that he was happy, and he hoped he would go soon home, in better shape.

They found JC a bed in the hospital, but I was not allowed to stay with him during the night. This wasn't good. I talked to the nurse in charge, but she was insistent about this. "Your husband will be fine. We will take care of him. He isn't at the end of his life; you can visit him tomorrow."

I hated her at that moment, but I felt better because she said he wasn't at the end of his life.

He was in a room with three other people. I assessed the situation, and I determined he would need a warmer blanket. I went home, gathered the winter blanket he loved, some pyjamas and toiletries, and I returned to the hospital. It was late, but they let me enter. I was heartbroken to turn home without him.

"I'll get better, and we'll still have years to be happy together," he assured me. "Go home. But come back tomorrow morning."

He looked better already after two bags of some liquid with vitamins had been pushed into his bloodstream.

I could not sleep at home. The house seemed to be missing its soul. I cried most of the night.

In the morning, a friend, Felicia, stopped by with flowers and a cake. Bloody hell, it was my birthday. I thanked her.

After she left, I ran to the hospital. I put in place all the tricks I knew to get JC to eat something.

Anda called me to visit her before I went home; she lived near the hospital. She treated me with the sausages I liked, made on the barbecue. We spent an hour outside in her garden, near the fire. She cheered me up a bit. She understood my bad mood; she knew it was not a happy moment. I told her what room JC was in in the hospital, but she never went to see him.

For a month, I spent more time near my lovely man in the hospital than at home. One day, I was happy he had some soup, and the next day I cried because I saw he was pretending to eat. He would chew the food, and when he thought I was not looking, he would spit it out into a paper or a napkin. I cooked everything I knew he liked, only to see him pushing it far from him on the bed table.

The previous two weeks in the hospital were very hard. JC accused me of wanting to keep him away when he wanted only to be at home.

In June, after more checks, the doctor told me that eight years prior, JC had a fall, and his brain was affected. Now, what was causing all this pain was blood affecting his brain. She told me my husband will not be with me for Christmas.

Shock took over. My chest felt like it was exploding. I couldn't stop the tears. I was filled with hatred—against the hospitals, doctors, nurses, and God…I was the angriest at Him.

Why? Why so soon? Why, when I was so happy? Why, when he was so happy? Why did God want him? Why was God so cruel to take my love? Why…

I needed to go out for a while; I didn't want to be seen by JC at that moment.

He wanted ice cream, so I went to a nearby supermarket. I was overthinking and crying. I entered the shop and grabbed the lollipops he liked from the freezer. Then I left the place, running back to him. I realised, when I gave him the pack, I had not paid. How could I be so crazy? I went back later. I explained, paid, and apologised for my mistake.

Before going home that night, my sweet love pleaded for me to take him home with me, "I don't want to die here; I want to be with you, at home." This was the first time he used the fatal word, 'die.' "TAKE ME HOME!"

The hospital set me up with a bed at home that suited his needs. Two days later, my love was home. Oh, God, he was so happy! He wanted to touch our flowers that he loved so much, so I took a pot with a geranium from outside and put it near his bed—which was now placed in the living room. Then he wanted to sit in the armchair and watch the lit fireplace. We stayed a long time near the fire. He was kissing my hand and caressing my head.

"I'll get better. I want to live," he told me, his eyes sparkling with happiness. "I don't like this bed; it still seems as if I am in the hospital. I am at home, aren't I?" (He was still confused because of the medication he took in the hospital.)

He took my hand and looked into my eyes, smiling. "I feel we are very happy together, my love. We are happy, aren't we? I feel I am the luckiest man in the world. I was blessed with you at a moment when I was sure life was finished for me. I must have done something good in my life…" His voice trailed off.

"Oh, yes, love, we are very happy together," I emphasized as I kissed his face and lips with all the love I was capable of in that hard moment.

After two days at home, I was convinced he would get better. He was reading his daily newspaper, drinking his Lucozade, and eating (though it was nothing compared to his appetite before the illness). He was very lucid, telling me lots of stories about his childhood and the war.

We laughed as before, but the intimacy was almost zero. JC would keep my hand in his for hours, and he would kiss me. But he was weak from losing lots of weight, so that was as far as it went.

Two weeks after he arrived home, he felt better. He looked really invigorated, and when I gave him an ice cream cone, he dripped it on my hand and ate it from there, slowly, making my body shake. It was erotic. He had a naughty look in his eyes. Then he kissed me in 'that' way. We both knew what this meant. We were looking into each other's eyes, and everything was back to normal for a moment, as months before. He continued to leak the ice cream on my hand, and I suggested to him, "We can put ice cream on my boobs so you can eat it better."

He jumped onto his bottom, ready to do this, his eyes bright and so, so, so happy. But in the next second, he started to cry like a baby. He knew for sure he could never do this again. We held each other for a long time. We both felt the love that kept us together for years. Neither of us wanted to cry so much, but we did. Feelings are feelings, wrong or not.

My father was also very ill. Lara and Lydia were with him for two weeks. He managed to have a video chat with me. I felt pain all over my body. He wanted to see me, and I promised I would be there soon.

"You are lying," he simply stated but with love.

I would not leave my husband now. I couldn't afford to be a second without him. If Dad died, I would feel guilty. I knew this, but I still chose my love. It was not really a choice for me; I could not do differently at that time.

Sometimes I got into my husband's bed with him. I would stay there, cuddling him, for hours. His nose rested on my head. I adored the way he smelled and the warmth of his body. I took to sleeping on the sofa, near his bed. I needed to be near him. His bed was only for one person, and I hated that.

I needed to call JC's son and give him the news. He would be in England the next month with his family, but I had the feeling it would be too late. He came in two days as he understood the urgency.

JC appeared happy, at peace with the world, but he still did not eat much. Now he wanted beer; I gave him a non-alcoholic one. He enjoyed it, even though it was zero alcohol. First thing in the morning, he drank one.

After one week, it was just the two of us again. I watched him dreaming during the night and listened while he was talking in his sleep.

I held his hand and kissed it. I kissed his beautiful face. I stayed near his bed, and I held him near me.

"You are the best thing that happened in my life. Thank you for all your love and care. Try to relax now. You've done the best for me; you can't do more," I told him.

Later, I couldn't talk, my throat was so dry. My heart felt like it was jumping out of the chest. My legs shook. I cried and cried and cried, sitting on the sofa when he was sleeping.

Johanna came to see me and brought a friend, Luana. She was a sweet girl and looked like a model. They tried to cheer me up. Johanna was helping me make JC more comfortable in bed. Her face showed she was preoccupied. She just kept smiling. After an hour or so, I felt a bit better, listening to these young girls chirping about their lives. Even JC was smiling, and he wanted to know Johanna's news; the gossip about Johanna and John. It was his way of pretending everything was normal.

On the fourth of July, Independence Day in the States, JC had been at home a month. He appeared in a good mood; he was reading his newspaper and wanted to watch TV. He was even hungry. He wanted strawberries and ate three with sugar, then he drank a coffee. I went to the kitchen and started to thank God for this moment. Maybe he would begin to eat more eventually. I danced around and jumped up and down. I checked on him again, and he asked for a beer. He also wanted to move from the bed to the armchair.

Thank God; thank you!

Now, I was happy to do some gardening. My flowers missed me. They needed a good trim. When I got to the potted tomato plants, which were under the living room windows, I waved to JC, and he waved back.

"I love you!" I shouted to him through the window.

Shortly, he called me in the house. He wanted to go to bed.

I helped him to get on his feet, held him in my arms, and moved him two steps toward the bed. I felt him falling, and I thought he was playing. When I saw his face though, I started to shake him and call his name out loud...***no, no, no, no, no, God, no...***

JC died in my arms. The most important person in my entire life disappeared. Gone in a split second.

I was the prima donna at the first violin performance in the concert of our lives. Now I was *nobody*. I was empty. Broken. I'd lost *everything*—the air I needed to breathe; the shoulder I went to cry on; the laughter that had filled our home; the only man who loved me with all his heart; the friend; the advisor; the teacher; the lover. I lost *my very heart and soul!*

I felt small and frightened. I was now alone in the world.

I was shattered, broken into millions of small shards and slivers of glass that could never be put back together the same way.

I would never be a part of *us* again. Us meant JC and I. I was half of a whole being. What would become of me now?

The pain in my chest was getting bigger. I could not feel my arms and legs. I gave JC the last kisses I could on this Earth.

My love, you are going somewhere else now. You'll have to meet God. Yes, God. Be kind to Him. I know you think 'nothing up and nothing down.' Maybe you'll be surprised. This life on Earth can't be all there is. You were full of laughs, happiness, intelligence, knowledge, and so much love. You did good in this life, and if there is an afterlife, you'll be well regarded. Try not to question God too much. Though I am sure you'll do it. You'll want some scientific explanations. Knowing you, maybe you'll even get some answers. The worse thing is I won't know any of this…until will meet again. The good thing is every day that passes will bring me closer to you…

That morning of the fourth of July, I was happy for the first time in the previous three months, thinking everything would be fine. I thought JC had started healing, and I hoped and dreamed. I had a big smile on my face, shadowed only by thoughts of my father's situation at home.

I called Johanna. She was at work, but Luana appeared after ten minutes. My sweet girl Johanna sent her representative to take care of me. Elena appeared also. As usual, she gave up everything to be near me when I needed her.

In a couple of hours, I was surrounded by friends. I didn't realise how lucky I was. My mind was clouded; I was half dead. I had seen them all, heard them talking to me, but I was far away, wrapped up in my misery. I remember voices, but no words. Ciel came a week later to stay with me for one month. God bless her!

My dad died from cancer two weeks after JC passed.

I hoped to be able to see him alive again, but I couldn't. Maybe it was better that I didn't see him ill. I will remember him as he was the previous summer: a bit forgetful, but well, and happy to have me there.

Within one month, I lost both 'the men' of my life…

> "Incredible change happens in your life when you decide to take control of what you do, have power over, instead of craving control over what you don't."
> Steve Maraboli

CHAPTER 10

The Three Steps towards Freedom

Maybe you recognised yourself in some of the situations from my life? Perhaps you've made some similar mistakes. We live hectic lives, these days, this is for sure. I said at the beginning, we live our lives with what we know. We may be overwhelmed by different situations, doing our best to solve problems as they appear. We struggle, and we think it is normal, that life is a dark path, full of pain and suffering.

What can we do differently? I'm sure you are eager to know.

It is all about our thinking. We have been told by our families that life is dreary, we need to fight a lot, and every event is created by us. They tell us to be good at school to get an excellent job in the future. Furthermore, we need a paramount social position and self-esteem to give us satisfaction. Society and the media tell us body image is vital because we need to show up on a cloud of perfection. We are told fear, comparison, and conflict (in both the workplace and family) are a normal part of our path in life. We start our lives knowing it will be tough.

We grow up as warriors, fighting the entire world to achieve happiness and to be seen.

When I was 13, my teachers used to tell me to fight more, to improve in sports and music, to get better grades—because I was intelligent but still not 'good enough.' Yet, I hated my music hours; I didn't have a musical bone in my body. And I hated sports classes as well. How do you improve something you don't like? With music, there wasn't much I could do when I simply was not designed for it. Regarding sports, I couldn't run more than 500 metres without feeling like I was dying. I was terrific in math, but who really cared? You must be perfect, in the eyes of others.

Later, I wasn't good enough for some of my boyfriends, or even for some of the people I considered friends. If you don't do what others want you to do, you'll be in trouble. Seems that everyone has a different measuring stick about perfection, friendship, school, and life, in general. Yet, there is a gigantic script to follow, the modern society script, full of indications about what is expected from us, these days, if we want to belong to the elite.

But is it essential to be perfect?

Louis Kahn, an American architect, once said, "Even a brick wants to be something. A *brick* wants to be something better. It aspires. Even a common, ordinary brick...wants to be more than it is. It wants to be something better than it is."

Buddha said, "All that we are is the result of what we have thought." I agree, entirely, with him. I wasn't like Kahn's brick, wanting to be something. I *thought* I was not good enough for this or that. I *thought* that maybe I didn't deserve too much. I *thought* I was not tall/thin/intelligent/brave enough. When my mother died, I *thought* I was to blame for not doing enough to help her or to be near her, despite realising I was still a child at the time.

I remember my first day of work, after university, as an accountant. I was thrilled to start this new adventure, but after one month, I wondered if I could be happy doing this all my life.

175

I couldn't picture myself working there, waiting for my annual leave once per year, being back to work after, doing the same annoying things again. "That's all?" I *thought*.

When I went to Italy, I *thought* life would change, and it would be better. I didn't realise that life was the same, no matter where you lived. You needed to do the same boring things if you wanted to pay your bills.

What I am trying to say is, we don't need to change jobs, lose weight, or move to another country to attain peace of mind. Our *thoughts* always go with us, and we make the same mistakes as before. Our mind creates the same movies in our heads, pain and grudges from the past will follow us, and fear of the future will reappear like before.

Moving to a new country the second time turned out to be a blessing for me, but this was my personal experience. I was blessed with the love of my life. This happened to be at a moment I was willing to change, ready for a mental transformation, prepared to make different choices. And to *think* differently.

It is effortless to live the way you know; it is safe for you in your comfort zone. New things may frighten you, even if you are unhappy with what or where you are at the moment. You live the same cycle: waking up in the morning with your *thoughts* about your (little or big) problems and going to bed with the same old luggage filled with your *thoughts*.

Considering my path of change, I have done some steps that helped me grow to be a happier individual. There are only three steps, but they were essential for my transformation:

1. I started with the lesson of forgiving things and people in my past.

2. I learned to love myself.

3. I became aware I needed more help, and I plunged into the infinite world of mindfulness.

Now you may think you know all this, or maybe you may wonder if this is enough for you to improve your life. These are the three steps I used; they mean everything to me. They transformed my life and freed me from my past grudges.

My mornings are now filled with gratitude for being allowed to see how beautiful the world is again, and meditation helps me to begin to unfold the day positively. I have trained my mind to forgive (but not to forget) myself for my wrong actions in the past and to forgive (but not to forget) others. I am willing to help without expecting something back, and I want people to be happy, to learn to love their lives. It would be beneficial to everyone, I think, to be more interested and aware of mindfulness, because meditating teaches our bodies to be aware of new feelings. It allows us to have a special moment with our thoughts and emotions. A moment from which our mind and body will benefit—a journey to getting healthier day by day.

1. Forgive the past

Getting out from the weight of the past is an important step. If you tell me it is easy, I will laugh! It took me two years to arrive where I am now.

My husband noticed I was sad after calling my father, and he naturally supposed this happened because I missed him, being so far from me. Of course, I was missing him, but I was sad because sometimes he was talking in the way he did after a glass of something. I couldn't be happy. How could I forget he was Bachus' friend?

Moreover, every time I went to visit him, we ended the visit by arguing, and badly. I loved and hated him at the same time. I spent so many tears thinking and rethinking the words he said to me, or I said to him. I broadcasted the films about our contradictions, so many times in my mind, I was exhausted and suffered health problems as a result. I ate when thinking, and my body suffered. My blood pressure went up and down. I was upset lots of the time, and I developed wrinkles on my forehead.

JC put me on the right path. He told me to concentrate on the present moment, to change my thoughts, because I was the only one with power over them. He explained that hating and overthinking these things wouldn't get me to a better place. I didn't consider his words too much then—I was numb to his teaching—but he planted a seed of forgiveness in my head. Then he kept watering this seed every day, and a little plant started to grow, despite my deafness.

JC told me to focus on the good Dad brought into my life. He was sure Dad had done lots of beautiful things for me. Otherwise, it would have been impossible to be as I was—the beautiful person who made JC so happy. Oh, yes, my love had a high regard for me, from our first days together. To him, I was a beautiful and intelligent woman who he was lucky enough to have by his side, especially at the end of his life.

I said I was reluctant at first to listen to him. But after considering, over time, what JC had said, somehow, sweet memories about Dad crossed my mind. I remembered how much he risked when going hunting for a wild boar or a deer, in a world that easily could imprison him for this action. I smiled, recollecting us on the riverbank, fishing, with Dad telling me about various Greek myths. Starting with Ouranos, the sky, and Gaia, his mother, the Earth, and continuing with Hera and Zeus, Prometheus, Eros and Psyche, Apollo, Diana and all the other deities I came to love so much. I could never hear enough about them.

I couldn't forget my father's patient side when helping me with homework in my first school years or when teaching me how to draw a landscape. Or the scary stories he invented ad hoc when Lara and I were too noisy, upsetting Mom. The long hours I watched him carving, amazed how his magic hands transformed distorted pieces of marble or wood into something full of life and meaning. The stories and thoughts came back to me freely because Dad was really fantastic in some ways.

He had his magic hat, with tricks for every situation, and he was there for us when we needed advice. Even now, thinking of him, I can see his smiling, intelligent face during a happy moment from his life. When he was taking care of his beautiful red roses in the garden in front of the house. I always smile about this sweet memory. I cherish this memory on a summer day when I miss him. I broadcast the film of that day again and again. I can feel the warmth of the sun and the roses' perfume in the air, and I can see, with my mind's eye, Dad explaining how to keep them growing so healthy.

This process of retrieving better memories of my father didn't occur in one day. I made friends with my feelings over two years, keeping calm when on the phone with Dad. Especially when I heard that voice that I didn't like. Instead, I would fight my mind from going in the direction of negative emotions. I understood positivity brought me the serenity I needed to clear up situations appearing to have no solutions. I trusted JC and the Universe, thinking kindly about my family problems. This process pushed me into a vortex of creativity, and I started to see things differently. I realized when other people, friends, mere acquaintances were in a stage of negativity in their life.

A word of caution here. If you are going to try to help when you have the desire to do so, choose to help people intelligent enough to understand what are you talking about. People who appear as the right candidate for a shift in their lives.

In my path towards happiness via forgiveness, I couldn't sit and watch colleagues at work hating each other. Especially about ephemeral little things produced by the movies generated from their negative minds or thoughts about a moment in time.

A young lady in one of my workplaces appeared very upset with the entire world. Nothing was satisfying her, and she complained to the manager about someone, almost every day. I became fed up with this, and I said, to myself, *"She needs some guidance and help."* So, I 'offered' my advice. A big mistake from my side. After days trying to persuade her to think positively and peacefully help others. After keeping calm and gentle with her, the manager called me to tell me what I said to her. The young lady had complained about me.

I had told her to go on the internet and find some books about thinking positively. And to check, on YouTube, some of the audio of Louise Hay or Abraham Hicks. I even told her maybe she would be happier if she was taking a course to help her to step into a better position at work. I asked her how she pictured herself at 40 when she was so harmful and bad to everyone now. I said she needed to change because she would be even more negative about everything, in time. But I was talking to a wall. She didn't want my advice. And she certainly didn't take any of it.

The manager was amused; she understood everything. I was sad about the situation. Some of us choose to stay, forever, in a dark place; some love to hate and criticise; some thrive on pointing out others' mistakes. If they don't find anything on the surface to use, they will dig until their sick mind is gratified. It is better to avoid these people; don't waste your time. Bless these people, wish them happiness, and let them go; don't dwell on them.

The last time I visited my father, it was a better week together. There was no resentment or hurt in my heart, and we both enjoyed every moment. We laughed and were happy. It felt so much better. For the two hour flight back to London, I analysed these new circumstances and decided it was the first time I said to myself, *"I am free from my past. Hurrah!"*

You'll never understand this feeling if you don't move from the angry things in your past. It is a huge milestone when you do this. It requires a shift of your mind, and it takes time, but it works. I know from my own experience: how hopeless I was feeling, and how incredible it felt when taking the first steps to think positively. The hard work I'd done slowly created satisfaction in me. And day by day life become lighter and more comfortable. I was free to enjoy the best time of my life with my husband, in love and with my own peace of mind. You only need to want it and to focus all of yourself in achieving it.

As Ann Bradford said, "Tell the negative committee that meets inside your head to sit down and shut up!" Try, every day, to be positive in everything. Even if you don't have enough money or a good enough job, or you have a problem that keeps you awake on the night—you need to smile the same, go to the mirror, look deeply into your eyes, and tell yourself that all is fine, you have what you need, you are lucky, and that things always work out for you, even if they don't appear to at the moment. Problems, whatever they are, don't get solved when you are angry because what you give out will return to you. Instead, you'll live in a circle of anxiety and frustration. Be brave, recognise your problem, but keep thinking that it will be okay, that you are strong, and your mind will get the right answer. Be willing to change.

2. Love yourself

What does it mean to love yourself? Ways you may think you love yourself: you nourish with food your body, you cover it in clothes, you put on makeup, and you leave your house only after a good look in the mirror. You check your health, and you see a doctor when needed. Some of you may go to a gym, a swimming pool, or a class, such as Zumba. But is that love for yourself or pure vanity?

Some of you may go to church on Sunday, or maybe your spirituality is in the form of meditating in the morning. Maybe you consider this self-loving.

Perhaps you don't care so much about your physical appearance or spirituality, but you criticise yourself for new and past actions.

Some of you may be stuck in a job you can't stand anymore, but you stay there out of fear, thinking you'll be rejected for a better one. You may think you are doing the right thing for yourself, after all, you can pay the bills.

And others may buy beautiful things—cars or properties or jewellery—telling themselves they are doing well, they love themselves, and they deserve this.

What makes *you* happy?

Maybe everything makes you happy at the moment, but the feeling is temporary. Cute clothes will only bring us a maximum of one week of happiness; we start to look for something new shortly after. A new car or a body shaped in the gym will fulfil our vanity for a while, but will we be truly happy? Going to the church will help for sure, but even after a confession, we may keep thinking of the bad things in our past. What we need a holistic approach—we need to cure the mind, spirit, and body—together.

My first days in England, with JC, must have been so strange for him. I was doing what I had done before. I had the 'poor me' moments: life is hard, I can't do this or that, I am not good enough to do this or that, I'm too old/unhappy/lonely/broken/fat. He couldn't believe I was so negative. He never studied mindfulness, but his mind was so healthy. He had colossal self-esteem, and when I asked him how he saw himself, he responded, very proudly, "I am a handsome and very intelligent man. I've always been very bright. Hahaha! I am old on the outside, but inside I feel like I am 21 years old."

He was happy every single day for the five years I was near him. (I am pretty sure he was the same all his life.) He thought every single morning was a blessed new day coming, one he should live to the maximum as tomorrow might never come.

And this handsome, brilliant man, was willing to help me to grow, to love myself, to be creative, to believe in my dreams, to forgive (but not forget) the past, and to be, simply, happy. The same as he was; the way he was.

When he asked me what my dream was, I said I wanted to write a book. This was what I wanted to do with all my heart, but at the time, I spoke limited English. I was convinced it would be only dream, forever. Yet here I am, finishing my book. I am a real-life example for those of you who don't believe enough to pursue your dreams. Everything is possible if you work at it, if you believe in yourself, if you push yourself, and, most of all, if you want it enough.

I started with English lessons on YouTube. I continued with courses for my job. I had more conversations. I watched hundreds of videos. And I read all kind of books (some that I'd found in my husband's library). Learning English took time and a willingness to improve my life.

I relaxed gardening, expressing my creativity in this way. Every summer, our back garden was our magical, colourful, mysterious world. Where we could hide from our daily problems, and where we connected with nature and nourished our souls.

If you want to love yourself, you must find something to be grateful for every day, treat people with respect, be patient, and support yourself in hard moments. You need to stop the comparison to others and accept what makes you different from them. We are all unique individuals; life is exciting because of our differences. Imagine a world full of people the same as you. You'd talk about the same things, you'd like or hate the same things, and you'd be bored to meet your friends, who were all the same as you.

Allow yourself to be what you are, with realism, because everybody makes mistakes. Learn to forgive yourself, become changed by kindness. Try to do good things, don't hurt others if you want good in your life. You will feel happier when you give back to others.

Live your life for you—no one else. You do not need to look for approval for every step you take. As I've said before, we are all different. Our points of view about life partly depend on our culture, our life experience, our age, where we were born, and our family background. Approval from others does not necessarily imply you are doing the right thing.

Step outside your comfort zone. (Your comfort zone is where you feel safe and protected.) You have to do more. Learning and growth do not happen within your comfort zone; it happens just outside it. You have to be willing to achieve a new goal, and celebrate it, big or small. Be proud of your growth.

Be brave. Eliminate from your life those 'energy vampire friends' who make you uncomfortable, who let you down, and criticise every step you do. You don't need them. Wish them good luck, and let them go, preferably far away from you. Keep people near you who encourage you, people who love and respect you, people who see in you as a fantastic friend.

3. Integrate mindfulness

When you are starting to get bored with your life, you need to get to the root of your problem(s). If you don't like the street you travel on, there must be something not quite right there. Louise Hay said in her book, *You Can Heal Your Life*, "The problem is rarely the real problem." Until you find the real problem, the root cause of what is plaguing you, you will forever search to solve inconsequential issues.

Some will need professional help. It is good to do this if you have the time, money, and desire.

Whether you solve your mind's puzzle on your own, or you seek professional advice, your success will rely on your willingness to make changes. Your goal is your total wellbeing. See yourself as that unique, beautiful person who deserves the best the Universe can give to you.

While seeking out your wellbeing, you'll have the choice to start with a physical, mental, or spiritual approach. Everyone begins the shift in one of these areas, knitting the pieces together eventually. Some will consider starting with better treatment for the body and/or eating healthier. Others will engage in therapy to address their mental issues. And someone else will plunge into meditation or prayer, helping with their spirituality. Where you start is irrelevant; take that first step.

It is essential to be aware of your condition if you want to heal it and stay on track. Keep challenging yourself and stepping out of your comfort zone. You'll have to fight strong resistance to moving forward.

Mindfulness is a psychological process. It involves patience and effort, but all the work on your thoughts will reduce stress, depression, and anxiety. It will bring your attention to the present moment, with no judgment involved. You will be able to experience the current moment entirely, aware of your feelings and bodily sensations, yet not caught up in their trickiness.

It is well known and demonstrated that mindfulness meditation brings changes in behaviours and health, at a physical and psychological level. Being mindful, focusing on the here and now, helps us to worry less about a dark past or an unknown and frightening future. It grows our self-esteem and gives us an easier way to connect with the outside world.

Depending on your goals or beliefs, you can work with a group under an instructor's guidance or learn meditation on your own. Today, we have tons of apps and books to follow. Or even YouTube. Resources are available.

My online business training gave me access to a platform offering lessons of meditation, with big names in the field as teachers. I was laughing at the beginning, considering meditation something childish, without a purpose—something stupid even. I didn't understand what it meant to stay still and quiet the mind. I didn't know what this was good for. But I dug deeper into the topic, thanks to my curious and knowledge-hungry mind.

Jon Kabat-Zinn, a known scientist, created a program known as "Mindfulness-Based Stress Reduction (MBSR)" and introduced it in clinics around the world. This approach to medicine helps to reduce stress and depression, as well as some problems related to anxiety. When anxiety is involved, it is better to have professional advice about the subject—somebody to guide you. We aren't able to do it all on our own.

Summary

Throughout this book, you have learned a bit about my life story—what situations and experiences made me who I am today. I've also given you three steps to help you deal with the things in your life that make you unhappy.

I was thrilled once I learned how to accept myself as I was, with all the mistakes I made, but not thinking more about them. I was better, not only with myself but with people around me in my life—friends and even false friends, the so-called energy vampires. We choose people to be friends with, but I am sure you have people in your life who you don't like very much; they are there, and they call themselves your friends. You let them be, but after half an hour together or on a call with them, you feel tired and drained. It is like they suck out all of your positive energy, leaving you fatigued and weary. Despite all the mindfulness that you nourish your mind with, and all the kindness that you have for the world, you feel as if your day would be better without these people. You want them to disappear from your life.

Keep going with your life. Focus on positivity. Forgive yourself or others for whatever you hate from your past. Hope. Take action. Surround yourself with people who consider you incredible—those who help you grow. Start to give yourself some of the love your heart is filled with.

I am not a specialist, and I didn't have significant issues to rectify. I needed some peace of mind. Starting mornings with meditation helps me to concentrate on 'now,' to accept my experiences (not judge them more), to make friends with my thoughts, to enjoy the day with all its moments—damaging and pleasant. To live a day where you can simply *be*.

I remember JC watching me, sometimes, rolling his eyes as I was a bit 'gaga' when he surprised me during my meditation.

"If you are happy, I am happy," he used to say. And we were.

At this moment, I am still grieving his death. I am hurt and sad, but my love for him will never die. He carved his place deep into my heart, and he will be there until my last breath.

Acknowledgements

I started dreaming of writing a book when I was five years old. At 44, I told my husband, JC, about my dream. He didn't understand why it was still a dream. Oh, JC, you were right about everything! If we want something, we need to do some work on it. I would like JC to be here physically—to thank him and to see his amazing blue eyes smiling. Thank you, my love. Always with me. Forever in my heart.

A big hug to my little friend, Paula Ciobanu—you are an astonishing friend. Thanks for the nights you lost staying near me, trying everything to make me smile, to forget. Thanks for encouraging me to write, to keep going, to be positive.

I cannot thank Crina Muresan enough; Crina who was near me in all the awkward moments of my life— patient, calm, and lovely.

Oana Hriscu, you are so sweet and kind; it is a pleasure to have you around. You and Paula are my precious girls.

Thank you, Andra and Lydia D'Addario, for your generosity and love for me. For giving me the help I needed to realise my dream. You are so far away, yet always present in my life. You are, and will both forever be in my heart.

I am grateful to my night manager, Von Andrew Garing, who gave me the time to finish my book. Thank you, Von.

Elena Presada, you are amazing with your positivity. You always send good vibes.

Lovella, you are great. So much help when I felt lost. I cannot thank you enough for everything.

I am grateful to so many others for their help: Simona Petrovan, Catalina Cosa, Oksana Polishchuk, Carmen Raliuc, and Lori Childers-Paoletti. You are amazing and positive people.

This book is no more a dream because somewhere in America, there's a beautiful person named Kary Oberbrunner, who is keen on helping people discover clarity and see their dream of becoming a published author come to fruition. Thanks to all the team at Author Academy Elite.

A big thanks to Dawn Thomas-Cameron, author and editor, for all your help and kind words. You are precious. I am learning lots from you.

C. James Crabbe, thank you for all the emotional and material support you still give me. You are your father's son! I am delighted you and your 'tribe' are my family. Love you all!

About the Author

D.G. Crabbe was born and raised in a land of beauty and mystery—in northern Transylvania, Maramures. Then she lived in Italy for 20 years.

A lover of languages and literature, she found herself instead with a degree in economics. Overwhelmed by bills to sort out, she dreams about seeing the world, travelling, and writing stories.

She didn't believe enough in herself until the day she met her soulmate. He encouraged her to pursue her love of writing.

Currently, she lives in England—in a fairy-tale cottage in Oxfordshire—the home where she found happiness near her beloved JC. She loves her beautiful garden and her trips around the countryside and works as a dedicated full-time health care assistant.

Printed in Great Britain
by Amazon

54051757R00118